TECHNICALLY, That's Illegal

TECHNICALLY, That's Illegal

an experiment in following the rules

Ann Sattley

© 2011 by Ann Sattley

Published by Lulu Publishing
Releigh, North Carolina

Printed in the United States of America

All rights reserved.

rubber stamp font on cover design supplied by Rebecca Simpson
front cover design by Ann and Matthew Sattley
edited by Matthew Sattley
eagle drawing courtesy of Jared Zuck
graphic art work by Matthew Sattley and Terra Reed

ISBN 978-1-105-01368-3

www.technicallythatsillegal.com

For my parents

who taught me that I could be whatever I wanted,
and proved they believed it by paying for my education.
I love you, Mom.
I miss you, Dad.

CONTENTS

Prepwork   1

Was Jack Handey Right?   5

My Friends As Lab Rats   11

My Turn in the Maze   49

Field Observation   75

Continuing the Experiment   104

Field Journal A   113

Field Journal B   116

Field Journal C   120

Field Journal D   124

Field Journal E   127

PREPWORK

I'm an eldest child. I've always had the inborn desire to please my elders, obey rules, and make people proud of me. While I can be abrupt, confrontation has never been a favored activity for me. So, regardless of the situation, I typically prefer to know what is expected of me and behave in accordance with the established guidelines.

At various times throughout my life, my desire to follow the rules has been embarrassing for me. When my husband and I were in graduate school, we moved into married student housing. At that time, it was an upgrade for us from our 10X50 trailer. Before we moved in, we were given a handbook and told to read it.

Being the obedient person I am, I did. Reading the handbook taught me that we were allowed to keep our little pets, two hedgehogs, since they resided in cages. However, as a condition on that, we were supposed to go into the office and get stickers to put on their cages. Evidently, I was the only person who ever read that handbook because they had no idea what I was talking about. Quoting the handbook and citing the page number only made matters worse. They eventually told me that I could keep my hedgehogs without the *required* stickers on their cages because, apparently, the stickers either could not be found, or they did not actually exist. This resolution did not come before I felt generally silly for trying to follow the rules and them communicating that they were a little put out by me telling them in so many words that they weren't doing their jobs. It's as if they didn't expect anyone to read the handbook. My attempt at being a good resident backfired from the get-go.

When I was in college, I read Henry David Thoreau's *Civil Disobedience*. I liked it, but it made me uncomfortable. I hoped an issue would never arise that would put me in the uncomfortable position of having to disobey the law, even though I agreed with Thoreau that governmental regulations should not override a person's conscience.

As I've gotten older, either the world is getting more unjust, or I'm finally paying attention. In either case, I've been made aware of things that have upset me and motivated me to write this book.

Please don't take this writing as a call to arms or a political action piece. This is simply a commentary on my recent observations concerning the evaporation of common sense in America. I was hoping that it would be largely comical, but I seem to have chosen a serious topic.

I didn't intend for this to be as scholarly or political as it is. Footnotes were never a part of the plan, but I can't seem to evict the academic in me. Plus I'm slightly worried that not giving copious citations will somehow get me into trouble. So, I err on the side of caution as usual. When an article is initially cited, the rest of the information about that story comes from that article until a new reference is made. It is formatted this way to avoid multiple references to the same source.

Referenced articles were all retrieved from the internet so readers can view the information on their own. Effort was made to ensure the most up-to-date information in each case. Often, however, the original story makes a big splash and the follow-up is difficult to locate. Please forgive any material that might be slightly out-of-date. That is one of the risks I run when writing a book about current events and laws.

It is my hope that some of the contents of the book surprise you, and I wouldn't be surprised if some things upset you. But, don't let any of it keep you from smiling and going about your business. As far as I know, that's not yet illegal, although my husband was once issued a bogus citation for *not* smiling while crossing a street in New Orleans. I still don't understand who that was or what that was all about, but I'm almost positive he wasn't doing anything illegal.

WAS JACK HANDEY RIGHT?

Absurdity makes Jack Handey funny. His *Deep Thoughts* include such irrational and unconnected topics as space aliens, Vikings, insects, movie ideas, reincarnation, and time travel.

Deep Thoughts were used on Saturday Night Live between 1991 and 1998 as segues between sketches. When read aloud on the show, I never thought they were funny. I don't know who read them, but they executed it in a serious tone and slow cadence that didn't move me. I forgot about them until a good friend bought me some of his books in an attempt to cheer me up during an extended stay in the hospital. When recited in a totally different manner, they gave me great pleasure.

My amusement from *Deep Thoughts* generally stems from the fact that they make no sense. The scenarios are so outlandish that, when imagined, usually result in laughter. One of my favorites is from his book *Deeper Thoughts;* it offers a useful tip on how to fit in with others at a party:

> *If you want to be the popular one at a party, here's a good thing to do: Go up to some people who are talking and laughing and say, "Well, technically that's illegal." it might fit in with what somebody just said. And even if doesn't, so what, I hate this stupid party.*

Even though I consider Jack Handey's trademark humor to be obvious in the quote, not everyone appreciates it, so I'll explain. Imagine this actually occurring. First of all, who possesses such social awkwardness that this strategy for striking up a conversation seems reasonable? Secondly, what are the chances that saying, "Technically, that's illegal" would actually mesh with the conversation?

This *Deep Thought* that used to make me laugh because of its absurdity has come up repeatedly in my mind over the last few years. I'm starting to think of it as almost prophetic in a way. It's not even funny to me anymore because it actually might be true.

I'm outraged with things these days. I don't mull on it all the time, but when I do, I get upset. Then, I take a deep breath and change the subject. The subject, however, continues to make its presence known. The issue here is that reasonable people are being threatened and punished because of stupid laws.

Sure, you might be annoyed with your neighbor because of their loud party or tall grass, and you may appreciate it when the town officials correct such infractions. The problem for me is that the code enforcement officers (whether they be police or other special officers hired by your city) that issue citations for these offenses are the same ones that are shutting down children's lemonade stands, garage sales, and the actions of Good Samaritans everywhere. These issues are covered in detail later in the book. For now, just consider the idea that, generally, people are reasonable and want to follow the rules. It's simply becoming harder and harder to do that.

The main problems I see with the current state of legislation and code enforcement in the United States, and even in small town America, are the following (all of which will be referred to throughout the book):

- Selective enforcement
- Unenforceable regulations

- Vague codes that can be interpreted to the liking of the person enforcing them
- Ultra-specific codes written in such a way that regular citizens have no way of knowing whether they're in violation or not
- Codes or laws that criminalize relatively normal or even benevolent actions
- Codes in place only for the convenience of those enforcing the law
- Codes meant to protect us from ourselves
- The assumption that someone in government has to fix our neighborly disputes
- The assumption that someone in government can keep us safe by amassing regulations
- Outdated laws that are now irrelevant and need to be taken off the books
- Ill-conceived reactionary laws that intend to prevent future crime after some tragedy has occurred
- Laws that constantly change, and the general public is not made aware of the changes

- Laws that are only in place to generate revenue for the government

The code enforcement department in my city has a Facebook page. Currently, it has 615 people who *like* it. Complaints about code violations in the city, complete with specific street addresses, riddle the wall of this page. It seems like a forum to complain about your neighbors using colorful language and degrading terminology. While I know that everyone wants to live in a nice town with clean neighbors, we should consider the impact of making numerous complaints and asking the government to come to our rescue.

I've always considered myself a law-abiding citizen. I don't take illegal drugs. I don't steal property. I use my turn signal. And, unlike some of the people stopping at the traffic signal I can see from where I sit, I even stay put during red lights where there's no traffic camera. But, the term *law-abiding citizen* is losing its meaning because everything is becoming illegal. I started to wonder if Jack Handey might be eerily and inadvertently right.

To test how deep this *Deep Thought* really is, I decided to do a couple of experiments. While I am not a scientist, I do know the steps of the scientific method. I have *observed* that Jack Handey's *Deep Thought* seems to be more relevant now than ever before. I *question* whether it is relevant in everyday conversations. My *hypothesis* is that it is. Then, I *experiment*.

For this experiment I want to pay attention to what types of things people are talking about and, without starting the conversation myself, take note of the topic at hand. I thought it might be interesting to see which of the things people naturally discuss could easily transition into a conversation about the legality of the topic. Secondly, I will experiment on myself by reading my town's municipal codes and writing about whether I am currently following them.

For the purposes of this writing, I obviously will not be reporting on every conversation that takes place during the scope of my observation time. Omissions will be made that are unknown to the reader. However, everything written in the next chapter was directly observed by myself and researched for its relevance to current laws and municipal codes throughout the nation.

You may be interested to know that you're probably breaking the law without realizing it. You're also almost certainly associating with a bad crowd of friends, as they are probably criminals, too. If you're curious about what it means to follow the rules, join me as I turn my friends into lab rats.

MY FRIENDS AS LAB RATS

The most logical place for me to conduct my social observation is on my social networking platform of choice – Facebook. A quick look at the status updates of my friends reveals several interesting topics.

Gardening

As I write, it's the middle of summer in the Midwest. At this time of year, talk about the family garden easily competes with conversations about baseball, health, and the weather.

As I look at my *Top News*, I see some updates about gardening. Various friends from Illinois to Michigan have recently posted pictures of their gardens. Others are posting pictures of their harvests. Yet others are discussing the canning they have been doing with the produce gleaned from their soil. These updates, and especially the pictures, tend to get quite a few comments from fellow gardeners and envious non-gardeners.

Both gardeners and non-gardeners would probably be surprised to know that what my friends and family are doing could, technically, be illegal. In Oak Park, Michigan, a woman was threatened with jail time of over 90 days for having a garden in her yard[1]. The problem with the garden, according to the city planner, is that it was in her front yard instead of the back yard. You see, technically, that's illegal.

The City of Oak Park, Michigan evidently has the time and resources to harass people trying to grow food. Yet they don't have enough resources to hold a fireworks display this year and their city employees' workweek was cut to four days from five to save money.

One might assume that this woman's vegetable garden must have been unsightly in order to deserve this citation. On the contrary, she had four raised plots that were very well maintained. A picture of the garden is shown on the link in the footnote.

In my opinion, the best part about her garden is that it is in the front yard, rather than the back. She indicated that she

---

[1] http://www.myfoxdetroit.com/dpp/news/local/julie-bass-of-oak-park-faces-misdemeanor-charge-for-vegetable-garden-20110630-wpms

intentionally planted it there so that her neighbors and their children could see it and become involved. In a day and age when there is little interaction between neighbors, this is refreshing.

The kicker in this situation is that nothing in the city code says you can't have a garden in your front yard. The vague code was just interpreted that way in this situation. Their code indicates that a front yard must contain "suitable, live, plant material." The garden is definitely live and definitely plant material. The problem here is a difference of opinion in what is *suitable*. Personally, I don't think anyone should have to go to jail or even court over a difference of opinion regarding a nebulous interpretation of a city code.

In the end, jail time for gardening can be avoided provided that you position your plot in accordance with the whims of city planners. However, depending on where you live, you might want to be careful about how you water your garden.

A few months ago, a friend made a blog entry about her recent acquisition of a rain barrel. This spiffy contraption was hooked directly to her home's downspout. The idea is that the barrel fills up and the water is saved and used for the garden in drier weather to avoid using city water for this purpose. This is a good idea from both an economical and environmental standpoint. While I've never owned a rain barrel, we've been known to do something similar here in the Sattley home. We sometimes put the water collected from our dehumidifier into the washing machine.

You might be surprised to know that the practice of rainwater collection is illegal in some Western states[2]. It is my understanding that several states have made provisions for small-scale collection if you register with the government[3]. Fortunately, my friend doesn't have to register with the government regarding her rainwater collection apparatus because she lives in Illinois. I'd better check into our practice of using the water from the dehumidifier for laundry purposes – I honestly wouldn't be shocked if it's somehow illegal.

A Toyota dealer in Utah butted heads with the law regarding his system of collecting large amounts of rain-water and using it in a new car washing system[4]. The law is in place to prevent those downstream from being denied water if those upstream hoard it. Even though we still rely on this directional water flow in rivers and streams to supply reservoirs, much of the water never makes it that far in dry states. Some states updated this law, but not without small-scale operations being required to obtain a water right from their local government. They own the water, you don't.

---

[2] http://www.rainwatercollecting.com/blog/2009/01/is-rainwater-collecting-really-illegal-in-some-states/

[3] http://www.ksl.com/?nid=148&sid=11414346

[4] http://www.ksl.com/?nid=148&sid=4001252

If you don't have a garden in the front yard and you don't water your garden with rain you've collected, don't assume you're off the hook yet concerning your garden. You also need to be careful in what you do with your produce. Definitely don't try to sell it without permission.

In Clayton, California, a children's produce stand was shut down because proper permits were not obtained[5]. In this case, the operation had been open for two seasons before it was shut down. The mayor indicated that it was shut down as a result of two residents calling the city to inquire about its legality.

Two common citizens, instead of buying melons from these entrepreneurial young ladies, decided to rain on their parade in a move to eliminate such audacious behavior. These girls, while apparently being guilty of violating zoning and health regulations, are also guilty of a little hard work and ingenuity. I suppose there have always been spoilsports, but it sure seems like people need to lighten up.

This situation touches on a couple of the current problems that I see. First of all, shutting down a child's vegetable stand is criminalizing a normal behavior. Ordinary, healthy children like to be productive. It helps them feel grown up and fosters a sense of responsibility. We should encourage this even if it might result in a two-minute blockage of our driveway. If they were inside playing

---

5 http://abcnews.go.com/US/story?id=5626065&page=1

video games all summer instead of tending their garden and making a little money, we would criticize "kids these days" for being lazy and lacking creativity.

These particular health and zoning codes are also selectively enforced. The article indicated that if the stand had only been up for a day or two, they would probably have turned a blind eye. But since it was open continuously throughout the harvest season, it was deemed unacceptable. In other words, they are admittedly not concerned about one of their stated reasons for closing the stand – health violations. It sounds to me like they only closed the stand to placate a few complainers.

In March 2009, an email circulated claiming that new legislation, the Food Safety Modernization Act, would ban gardens and put organic farmers out of business.[6] While much of the email was false, there are still some troubling facts to face within this bill. While it's true that it doesn't contain any language referring to banning back yard gardens, it could force small, family-owned farms to follow the same regulations as large-scale operations, which would be financially unfeasible for many.

This bill was eventually passed by congress and is now the law of the land[7]. The main problems with the bill are that it is

---

6 See http://www.snopes.com/politics/business/organic.asp for more information

7 http://www.gpo.gov/fdsys/pkg/BILLS-111s510es/pdf/BILLS-111s510es.pdf

reactionary, assumes governmental responsibility over personal choice, and will most likely be selectively enforced.

It is generally assumed that the Food Safety Modernization Act was drafted as a response to several food contamination incidents, including the peanut-related *Salmonella* outbreak of 2009. Everyone agrees that it is important to keep consumers safe. But, we don't need reactionary laws in order to accomplish that. The fact that thousands of people got sick from *Salmonella* in the peanuts was tragic. However, if it was preventable, it wasn't because there weren't enough regulations. We need to keep in mind that it is already in the farmers' best interest to make safe products[8]. Their bottom line depends on it, and money talks.

One of the issues addressed in the Food Safety Modernization Act is raw (unpasteurized) milk. While this legislation doesn't affect the family garden, it does address the issue of personal choice in health-related matters. The Food Safety Modernization Act allows the federal government to ban the sale of raw milk. Consuming unpasteurized milk does come with risks, specifically pathogenic microorganisms like *Salmonella*, *E. coli*, and *Listeria*[9]. However, some claim health benefits from drinking raw milk that are not recognized by the Food and Drug

---

[8] http://www.reuters.com/article/2009/03/31/us-peanut-plantings-idUSTRE52U3K720090331

[9] http://www.fda.gov/Food/ResourcesForYou/Consumers/ucm079516.htm

Administration. Whether the milk is good for you or not isn't the issue. The salient observation here is that the government is putting itself in a position to make that decision for you. As soon as that happens, you can say "goodbye" to kids selling sweet corn in the parking lot.

Yard Sales

Like the family garden, this is also the time of year for yard sales. People flock to these sales and show up early in the attempt to find the best deals, the missing piece of their collection, some treasure, or the perfect gift. People brag about the bargains they found. Several of my friends have recently posted pictures of items they intend to offer for sale at an upcoming yard sale. Maybe I should show up at their yard sale and say, "Technically, that's illegal."

One of the main attractions at any yard sale is baby items. Baby supplies are expensive and quickly outgrown, which makes used items very appealing to many parents and grandparents. However, since the items may have been recalled, many used baby items are illegal to sell thanks to the Consumer Products Safety Improvement Act[10].

Illegal recalled items influence the sale of baby supplies. Anything you plan to include in a yard sale must be crosschecked

---

10 http://frwebgate.access.gpo.gov/cgi-bin/getdoc.cgi?dbname=110_cong_bills&docid=f:h4040enr.txt.pdf

with the Consumer Products Safety Commission's (CPSC) database of recalled items. These items range anywhere from toys to household products to sports equipment and other miscellany. The database contains literally thousands of recalled products. A quick and random look reveals such items as IKEA mattresses[11], Hayes Company outdoor candles[12], Yamaha ATVs[13], and Coby portable DVD players[14]

The CPSC has published a poster that warns of death and injury from recalled items and asks those hosting yard sales to "make safety their business[15]." Whatever happened to the old adage *Buyer Beware*? Where yard sales are concerned, we are now implementing the *Seller Beware* strategy in America and anyone trying to make a few bucks and de-clutter their space is being subjected to the same standard as the companies who manufacture the items.

Admittedly, the federal government has not, to my knowledge, hired undercover agents to roam your neighbor's yard sale and check for illegal items. It's almost laughable to think about this occurring, and that's part of the problem. If the federal government is going to bother banning the sale of recalled items

---

11 http://www.cpsc.gov/cpscpub/prerel/prhtml09/09331.html
12 http://www.cpsc.gov/cpscpub/prerel/prhtml07/07304.html
13 http://www.cpsc.gov/cpscpub/prerel/prhtml10/10733.html
14http://www.cpsc.gov/cpscpub/prerel/prhtml10/10205.html
15 http://www.cpsc.gov/nsn/yardsales.pdf

and specifically note yard sales in its efforts to keep us safe, they need to be able to enforce it. If it's unenforceable, it's meaningless.

I think I would be hard-pressed to locate a single American who bothered to crosscheck each of their garage sale items with the CPSC's database. As far as I can tell, it's already a lot of work to sort, tag, and display the items. On top of that, there's the signage that needs to be in place for advertising purposes.

If you're planning to have a yard sale, and you don't live on a busy street, the best thing to do is to place a sign at a busy intersection that points the way to your sale or gives the address. In fact, many garage sale goers simply drive around and look for these signs. But, technically, they're probably illegal, too.

In Oskaloosa, Iowa police officers and street department officials are actively removing garage sale signs[16]. Telephone poles can get pretty beat up, and too many old staples and remnants of signs that were never taken down eventually cause an eyesore. But, in this case, they are also banning signs from being placed between the street and the sidewalk because that's city property, too. The only place signs are allowed is on your own property or on your neighbor's property if you have their permission. So, if you live on a dead-end street, your only legal advertising options are to pay for space in the newspaper or to advertise online. The

---

16 http://oskaloosa.com/local/x1376630878/Police-Illegal-garage-sale-signs-must-go

newspaper article was quick to point out the option of advertising with them.

Common sense would tell us that the signs (particularly the lawn signs since they don't damage poles) should be allowed if they are promptly taken down at the conclusion of the sale. Political signs can still be placed in such areas in most towns. In Oskaloosa, so far, they are just removing the garage sale signs, but since the signs point to your house and most-likely give your address, it would be simple for them to identify the perpetrator in order to fine them the next time they find an illegal sign. This course of action was indicated as a possibility in the future. I'd take them seriously. After all, you don't want an officer showing up at your sale even to issue a warning. Once they see all of those recalled items you have for sale, you'll be in big trouble.

Having a yard sale is also illegal if you happen to do it more than a few days per year. Most municipalities, mine included, regulate this sort of thing to discourage people from setting up veritable flea markets in their yards. It's a good idea, but like many regulations, not reasonable when enforced.

A woman in Salem, Oregon was told to shut down her yard sale that had been going for a few consecutive weekends[17]. City officials used the *rules are rules* excuse for shutting her down. So, what's the big deal? The big deal is that the woman is dying of

---
17 http://salem.katu.com/news/news/442449-womans-yard-sale-pay-medical-bills-gets-shut-down

bone cancer and is using the yard sale to pay her medical bills since she is too ill to work. She even moved her yard sale to the back yard to avoid being a nuisance. But, a neighbor complained, and that's all it took to cut off a woman's sole source of revenue. If she continues to operate the yard sale, she faces a misdemeanor charge and a fine of up to $300. Maybe she should have all of her medical bills forwarded to the neighbor who complained.

Walking to School

It's the end of July. Summer is more than half over for the school age youth of America. Mild complaints by some of my younger friends about having to return to school are already popping up on my Facebook wall. Back to school sales are probably already in full swing at many retail outlets. Heck, they might even be over by now since it seems like I'm always behind a season or two at the store.

The recent resurgence of the topic of school reminds me of some of last year's comments. One of my friends was asked by her local school district not to allow her son to ride his bike to school before a certain age (I think it was eight) even though they live fairly close to the school. At that time, I was kind of surprised by the rule. I don't remember how old my brother was, but my parents made him bike to school once when he was given Saturday detention. Our school was about seven miles from home. I don't think he ever got Saturday detention again.

In most places, allowing your children to walk to school is not illegal. But, apparently it is in South Jordan, Utah[18]. One mother received a citation by an officer who saw her kindergartener walking home unaccompanied. The citation was for misdemeanor child neglect.

Her son used to ride the bus to school, but the route was eliminated. The district is unable to hire crossing guards, which she has requested at meetings. The boy was wearing a reflective orange vest at the time the officer picked him up. Does she sound like a neglectful parent to you?

Regardless of whether allowing your child to walk to school should justifiably result in a ticket, it definitely makes you guilty in the court of public opinion these days. Some parents allow their children to walk to school in order to instill independence in them. Even if police officers never pick them up, children walking to school unaccompanied will certainly raise a few eyebrows amongst other parents. While some concerned parents file police reports of unaccompanied children, others follow the kids to make sure they arrive safely. Judge these three things on the creepiness factor from a child's perspective: Getting picked up by the police, being followed by a stranger, or walking to school?

---

18 http://www.deseretnews.com/article/705363083/South-Jordan-mom-cited-for-neglect-for-allowing-child-to-walk-to-school.html?pg=1

In the late 1960s, over 40 percent of children walked to and from school (in the snow and uphill both ways, no doubt). In 2001, it was less than 13 percent[19]. I would venture to guess that this number is even less 10 years later.

In this age of concern for the environment, it would be sensible and consistent to encourage less driving. Instead, we have transitioned from walking to driving.

> *Experts say the transition has not only contributed to the rise in pollution, traffic congestion and childhood obesity, but has also hampered children's ability to navigate the world[20].*

Maybe we should be following, reporting, and citing those who drive their kids to school instead. Just kidding. We have enough laws.

In their defense, many people who see unaccompanied children are only trying to help. They are concerned about safety. We have been programmed to be concerned about safety. We have also been programmed to believe that all accidents can be avoided and that safety can be legislated. As long as we maintain this flawed mindset, the government will continue to enact laws that

---

19 http://www.nytimes.com/2009/09/13/fashion/13kids.html?pagewanted=1&adxnnl=1&adxnnlx=1311707751-ZYH84hzHm%20k8iWNiymoTxQ

20 http://www.nytimes.com/2009/09/13/fashion/13kids.html?pagewanted=1&adxnnl=1&adxnnlx=1311707751-ZYH84hzHm%20k8iWNiymoTxQ

restrict our freedoms and wind up labeling responsible, involved parents as *neglectful*.

Unhealthy Food

In addition to being garden season, yard sale season, and back to school anxiety season, it is also carnival season. I went to a carnival last year for the first time in a few years. Even though it was my first appearance in a while, nothing much had changed. It was still a place to run into people you nearly forgot about, and also the place to go for indulgent food choices.

I have a friend who seems to be obsessed with funnel cakes (who isn't?). In the last week or so, he has made several posts and status updates on the topic. We didn't have funnel cakes at county fairs where I grew up – we had elephant ears. They're very similar. Both are made when batter is poured into boiling cooking oil[21]. They are typically served with confectioner's sugar or a cinnamon-sugar combination. Also, they may be illegal where you live, depending on how they're cooked.

Cooking with trans fats is illegal in a few places throughout the United States. Please don't assume that I think trans fats are good for you. But, also, please don't go to the carnival and expect to get healthy food. The debate here isn't whether trans fats and the foods cooked in them are healthful choices. The debate is over whose job it is to keep us healthy.

---

21 http://en.wikipedia.org/wiki/Funnel_cake

As long as the government considers it their job to keep us healthy, there will continue to be restrictions on our choices. In an attempt to preempt government regulations on their industry, McDonald's restaurants are now cutting the amount of fries given in a happy meal and substituting them for apples[22]. Even though customers already know that apples are an option in the meals, only 11 percent of customers were making that choice. McDonald's is giving all the kids apples even though 89 percent of them may not get eaten. This is particularly devastating to me because I will now have to share more of my fries with my kids.

It seems to me like the government doesn't trust us to make good decisions on our own. Instead, they want us to trust their guidelines, recommendations, and regulations to keep us safe and healthy. While they don't trust us, I'm beginning to wonder if we should trust them.

In the 1940s, the (United States Department of Agriculture (USDA) introduced a food wheel that recommended individuals eat something from each of seven food groups a day[23]. One of the seven groups was butter and fortified margarine! At the bottom of the wheel were the words, "In addition to the basic 7...eat any other foods you want[24]." I wonder if that includes funnel cakes.

---

22 http://hosted.ap.org/dynamic/stories/U/US_MCDONALDS_HAPPY_MEAL_CHANGES?SITE=AP&SECTION=HOME&TEMPLATE=DEFAULT&CTIME=2011-07-27-00-54-46

23 http://en.wikipedia.org/wiki/History_of_USDA_nutrition_guides

24 http://en.wikipedia.org/wiki/File:USDA_-_Basic_7_Food_Groups.jpg

After the food wheel was discontinued, we went to the basic four food groups of vegetables and fruits, milk, meat, and cereals and breads. Then, these groups were represented in pyramid form starting in 1992 so that we would know how much of each group to consume. Grains made up the base of the pyramid, symbolizing that we should consume about twice as many grains as items from any other group[25].

Then, in 1992, an updated pyramid was created and marketed to us. This time, the space for the grains only took up slightly more room than the vegetables and no information was given about how many servings of each group we should consume[26]. Most recently, the pyramid was completely discontinued in favor of a plate design[27]. This depicts the portion of the plate that should be devoted to each food group at each meal.

The USDA is starting to confuse me. In an attempt to be clear, they have succeeded in cutting almost all substance from their message. A person used to be able to look at the food pyramid and get some relevant information, such as which foods are in each group and how many servings of each group we should eat. Now, we get a cryptic, geometric picture of a plate with almost no substantive information.

25 http://en.wikipedia.org/wiki/File:USDA_Food_Pyramid.gif
26 http://en.wikipedia.org/wiki/File:MyPyramidFood.svg
27 http://en.wikipedia.org/wiki/File:USDA_MyPlate_green.jpg

The USDA isn't the only branch of government that is trying to keep us healthy. There's also the Food and Drug Administration (FDA). Among other things, the FDA is responsible for:

> *Protecting the public health by assuring that foods are safe, wholesome, sanitary and properly labeled; human and veterinary drugs, and vaccines and other biological products and medical devices intended for human use are safe and effective[28].*

Good thing we have the FDA on our side. If we didn't maybe millions of people would still be taking the drugs they approved and then recalled, like Vioxx and Fen-Phen.

The FDA operates as an arm of the United States Department of Health and Human Services (HHS). The stated goal of HHS is for "all Americans to live healthier, more prosperous, and more productive lives[29]." As part of this goal, they have rolled out a big new campaign on, of all things, fatherhood[30]. Their new fatherhood website (www.fatherhood.gov) is heavily promoted. I only know about it because of radio promotions. So, if you're not already upset about government intervention in our food choices,

---

28 http://www.fda.gov/AboutFDA/Transparency/Basics/ucm194877.htm
29 http://www.hhs.gov/about/
30 http://www.fatherhood.gov/about-us

now they are trying to tell men how to be parents. Please note that there is no equivalent www.motherhood.gov.

So maybe we shouldn't trust the USDA because of constantly changing information. And maybe we shouldn't trust the FDA because they sometimes approve dangerous drugs. Where else can we turn? I don't know about you, but I'm going to the fair for a deep fried Oreo to think about this problem.

If you don't like funnel cakes or anything else cooked with trans fat, you're not exempt from the food crusaders. There are current assaults on other food items, including soda pop and salt. The salt crusade is particularly outrageous because its scientific basis is shaky (pun intended)[31]. Here's a quote from a recent article in Scientific American entitled *Its Time to End the War on Salt*:

> *The American Journal of Hypertension found no strong evidence that cutting salt intake reduced the risk for heart attacks, strokes or death in people with normal or high blood pressure. In May European researchers publishing in the Journal of the American Medical Association reported that the less sodium that study subjects excreted in their urine – an excellent measure of prior consumption – the greater their risk was of dying from heart disease.*

---

31 http://www.scientificamerican.com/article.cfm?id=its-time-to-end-the-war-on-salt

The *American Journal of Hypertension* article referenced in the quote was not just a single study – it was a meta-analysis of seven studies. Most of us have been told our whole lives that salt intake is bad for us, so we accept it as fact. Current research is chipping away at that foundational tenet of our health education. If the jury is out on this issue, maybe we shouldn't be so quick to make it illegal. That doesn't stop the FDA, who plans to gradually mandate the reduction of sodium in foods[32].

Besides the big debates on trans fat and salt, the government is also waging war against another common health assailant – lemonade. Children's lemonade stands are being fined and/or shut down by police across the country for violating municipal codes and dispensing food without a permit to do so[33]. Without government regulation of the lemonade, there is a risk that it could be unsafe to consume.

As was the case with the children's vegetable stand, these kids weren't harming anyone, and the police didn't just succeed in closing down a lemonade stand. They also succeeded in discouraging industriousness. If I see a lemonade stand, I plan to make an effort to pay them a visit and staying to chat a while. After

---

[32] http://www.washingtonpost.com/wp-dyn/content/article/2010/04/19/AR2010041905049.html?hpid=topnews

[33] http://www.foxtoledo.com/dpps/news/offbeat/police-in-ga-shut-down-girls-lemonade-stand-nt11-jgr_3881739

they let down their guard, I'll be sure to gather a little bit of information on the perpetrators and call the police.

In all seriousness, though, kids often think of things like this as ways of generating revenue – and it's far better than whining and begging without doing any work. The article I previously referenced was about kids who were trying to raise enough money for the admission fee at a water park. And, then there's the story of the boy in Michigan who started a lemonade stand to help his parents pay for his sister's funeral[34]. I'll bet nobody had the guts to shut that one down.

At one point in our history, the government succeeded in passing an amendment to the U. S. Constitution that banned alcohol within our borders[35]. The *prohibition* led to much underground crime and did almost nothing to curb behavior. When will we learn our lesson? If we're not careful, we'll have black market cookie and pickle shops before you know it.

Home-Based Religious Studies

I told myself that this book wouldn't get too political or religious. Well, too bad. Since this experiment involves naturally observing my friends' conversations and some of my friends happen to be Christians, the subject was bound to arise.

---

34 http://www.wxyz.com/dpp/news/region/macomb_county/boys-starts-lemonade-stand-to-help-parents-pay-bills-following-sister%27s-funeral

35 http://en.wikipedia.org/wiki/Prohibition#Prohibition_in_the_United_States

This week, one of my friends was commenting that they want to get more involved with a Bible study. Another friend mentioned that they were enjoying their weekly ladies' Bible study. My husband and I have used our home as a gathering place for a small group Bible study in the past. This is commonplace amongst Christians.

Many people with religious beliefs enjoy gathering with like-minded individuals for study, prayer, and fellowship. Indeed, this is how the Christian church began. There were no church buildings in early Christianity – only the homes of those willing to share their space with others. For a variety of reasons, some modern believers reject churches in favor of these home gatherings.

In these home gatherings, some claim you can be more authentic and honest about your faith because the setting is natural. Rather than paying an official person to talk to you every week, these gatherings generally rely on group involvement. But, in some places, they're illegal.

Holding a Bible study at home without a permit is illegal in San Diego County, and it might be illegal in your town, as well. In 2009, a man and wife were told that they could not continue to have weekly meetings in their home unless they got the proper permit, which would cost them tens of thousands of dollars[36].

---

36 http://www.foxnews.com/story/0,2933,522637,00.html?test=latestnews

They were warned in writing that without the permit, they were using their own land unlawfully.

After this story became famous around the globe, San Diego County changed their tune. They decided that the couple didn't need a permit after all. Presumably, if this story hadn't gotten airplay on major news networks, this couple would still be enduring harassment for doing something *illegal*.

One of the reasons this story got the attention it did is because it wasn't originally presented to the couple as a parking or zoning violation, but a religious issue. The issue in San Diego was the illegal *religious assembly*. Religious freedom restrictions rightfully tend to draw a lot of attention and debate in this country. Only after people became outraged by the story did the county government change its tune and start discussing the parking issue.

The restriction in this case hearkens to commonplace incidents in China. Christianity has been growing in China for some time now, but if a church fails to register and be officially recognized, they face persecution[37]. That sounds a lot like the case of the basic home Bible study in San Diego to me.

---

37 http://en.wikipedia.org/wiki/Christianity_in_China

Good Deeds

Unfortunately, 2011 has been the year of the natural disaster[38]. There has been flooding and cyclones in Australia, landslides in Brazil, an earthquake and tsunami in Japan, an earthquake in New Zealand, flooding in the southern United States, and tornadoes in Joplin, Missouri – among other things.

As these events have transpired, many people have given their time and resources to aid the victims of these disasters. Some of my friends have made trips to and from Joplin recently to help with relief efforts.

One of the problems I mentioned earlier with over-legislation is the fact that many laws and codes purport to have our best interests in mind, but they wind up hurting people.

Take the case of Westgate Tabernacle Church in West Palm Beach, Florida, for example. In 2008, they put up a tent on their property and allowed homeless people to sleep in it[39]. They should have known beforehand not to do something nice like that. It's illegal, you know.

In this case, code enforcement officers said that the tent violates county building codes. The church was cited and warned

---

[38] http://www.msnbc.msn.com/id/43727793/ns/world_news-world_environment/#

[39] http://articles.sun-sentinel.com/2008-08-05/news/0808040446_1_tent-code-enforcement-shelter

that they could face fines of up to $1,000 a day if the tent was not removed.

Prior to erecting the tent, this church was already housing homeless people inside its walls. When the need became too great, the tent was placed on the property. Up to 55 men sleep in the tent on any given night. In a community where there is obviously a need for shelter, leave it to the government to discourage citizens from getting involved.

I suppose the problem here is that the tent and its residents are unsightly. Nobody wants to see homeless people hanging about. Perhaps it would be better if they were scattered in dumpsters or under bridges rather than being congregated together like that.

If you want to help homeless people in West Palm Beach, I guess you have to volunteer at the local homeless shelter, instead. But, wait – there isn't one. That's the problem. The pastor of Westgate Tabernacle Church has stated that he will act in civil disobedience by leaving the tent up "until there is no longer a need for it," which means "until the county builds a shelter or Jesus comes".

It's not as if the church is just trying to be defiant. They even offered to move the tent to city property where there wouldn't be a zoning conflict. The city denied this request because tents are not allowed for sleeping purposes in any of the city's zones. I suppose it's better to do nothing at all for the homeless than to put up a tent.

It is truly a sad state of affairs when a Good Samaritan comes against governmental opposition for doing an admirable deed and meeting the needs of people in his community. If he ignores the county's regulations, this is definitely a case of warranted civil disobedience. Maybe people in this church actually read and acted on the words of their sacred text:

> *When the Son of Man comes in His glory, and all the holy angels with Him, then He will sit on the throne of His glory. All the nations will be gathered before Him, and He will separate them one from another, as a shepherd divides his sheep from the goats. And He will set the sheep on His right hand, but the goats on the left. Then the King will say to those on His right hand, 'Come, you blessed of My Father, inherit the kingdom prepared for you from the foundation of the world: For I was hungry and you gave Me food; I was thirsty and you gave Me drink; I was a stranger and you took Me in; I was naked and you clothed Me; I was sick and you visited Me; I was in prison and you came to Me.'*
>
> *Then the righteous will answer Him, saying, 'Lord, when did we see You hungry and feed You, or thirsty and give You drink? When did we see You a stranger and take You in, or naked and clothe You? Or when did we see You sick, or in*

> prison, and come to You?' And the King will answer and say to them, 'Assuredly, I say to you, inasmuch as you did it to one of the least of these My brethren, you did it to Me.'
>
> Matthew 25: 31-40, New King James Version

Maybe the words of Jesus need a little modern twist. Maybe something more like this (please read as sarcasm and accordingly forgive my blasphemous tone):

> *You know I have said that the greatest commandment is to love the Lord your God with all your heart, soul, mind and strength and the second greatest commandment is to love your neighbor as yourself. When I come back and it's judgment time, everyone will gather around. I will separate the good people from the bad ones. A good person is kind to their neighbors by keeping their lawns tidy and not driving down the value of the surrounding houses. Good neighbors don't keep anything unsightly on their property, including less fortunate people. Bad people are those that ignore city ordinances and jeopardize the health and safety of everyone.*

One year on Christmas Day, my brother and I drove downtown and worked in a soup kitchen. On a day when everyone we knew was being showered with presents, this was an educational and humbling perspective for us. I remember feeling extremely fulfilled when I helped these people even though I was doing dishes on Christmas. It was more memorable than any gift I received that year.

Imagine how rewarding it would feel to know you're helping to feed a person that otherwise wouldn't get a meal. A couple in Houston, Texas made it their business to do that. For more than a year, they fed homeless people in their city. But, the city made them stop because they were running an illegal operation[40].

In this case, the problem was that the couple didn't have a permit to distribute food. You see, without a food permit, the safety of the food could not be verified and a homeless person might get sick (nevermind the fact that people frequently get sick from eating at restaurants that do possess food permits). Alternatively, I suppose a homeless person might look around for food, not find any, and steal to feed their kids. I can't imagine any homeless person refusing a home-cooked meal because of the possibility that it might make them sick. It sure is a good thing the homeless have the city of Houston on their side since they surely can't count on their own judgment to keep them safe.

This law, which is designed to protect the general public from food-borne illness in restaurants, has reached into private charities and actually contributed to the problem of hunger on the streets. This is a classic case of the code attempting to protect us

---

40 http://www.chron.com/disp/story.mpl/metropolitan/7381016.html

from ourselves and criminalizing benevolence in the process. If we're not careful, we're going to scare off all of the humanitarians.

After a tragedy in his life, an Illinois man was inspired to help make a difference in his community. After a drunk driver killed his friend, he had the idea to start a free ride service for those too intoxicated to drive. He operated this service for three years before he was arrested for it[41]. It's illegal in Quincy, Illinois to give rides to people who would otherwise dangerously attempt to transport themselves home. I guess he should have known better.

It actually wasn't illegal to do this until the taxi drivers in the town complained that he was operating a taxi service without an appropriate license. Up until the complaint, a taxi license was only required if the service was *for hire*, and since he was operating a free service, he didn't require a special license. The city council actually changed the language of the statute to make his service illegal.

This man, a died-in-the-wool altruist, was twice arrested (at the time the article was written) because he refused to stop offering the free rides. I wonder if the real taxi companies actually make more money while he's in jail. My guess is probably not. I expect there are just more drunks driving around Quincy and the surrounding area.

---

41 http://jalopnik.com/5604559/how-one-good-samaritan-was-arrested-for-driving-drunks-home?skyline=true&s=i

The reality is that Americans are generous. When disaster strikes around the globe, people can generally count on Americans coming to help with disaster recovery efforts[42]. Americans also give generously to charity even if they don't help with their hands. So, nobody should be surprised when passers-by feed a stranger's parking meter. But, in many places, that's illegal. They don't want people to follow the rules by keeping their meters fed. They want to give them tickets for not following the rules. They get more money that way.

Eugene, Oregon is one of the places that forbids people from feeding strangers' parking meters[43]. One man was even fined $810 after a confrontation with a ticket writer that started because he was feeding expired meters. There is some discrepancy in the story regarding how the incident transpired, and the offender may not have acted with complete decorum, but the fact remains that there is a law on the books in Eugene, Oregon that forbids a person from feeding other people's parking meters.

What about other people's wallets? What would you do if you found someone's wallet on the street? This happened to my friend. She did the right thing and turned it in to the nearest police station. Unfortunately, she was treated like a crime suspect. They asked for her identification and began to run checks on her in

---

[42] http://www.patheos.com/Resources/Additional-Resources/Are-Americans-Generous?offset=0&max=1

[43] http://kezi.com/news/local/158928

their computer system. Evidently, the police in her town use every opportunity to catch people with outstanding arrest warrants – including kind-hearted, good people that are returning lost items. I suppose there may have been the off chance that a wanted felon would turn in a lost wallet, but not anymore. They've now learned that it would be best for them to just keep it.

Much to my dismay, the cynical phrase *no good deed goes unpunished* is starting to resonate true in our society. I only hope that those attempting to assist victims of the recent natural disasters don't encounter this much nonsense when they attempt to bring aid in those unfortunate circumstances.

Photography

Summer is a great season for taking pictures. Seniors are getting their pictures taken just prior to the start of their final year in school. Tons of people are getting married and getting their big day immortalized in pictures (while the guests are hot and starving at the reception hall, no doubt). Families are taking long vacations and publishing their pictures online for everyone in the Midwest to drool over.

My eldest son turned two earlier this summer. A friend took his pictures. In May, my youngest son was born. We had his pictures taken, too. We weren't planning on buying many of the pictures taken by the hospital-provided photographer, but they sucked us in by taking a wonderful shot of our baby boy.

Photography is a hobby enjoyed by many people. Unfortunately, it's becoming illegal. When some men went to Phoenix, Arizona to take cityscape pictures, they became the focus of a Homeland Security investigation[44]. An officer claimed that the two were suspiciously taking pictures of a federal building.

In addition to federal buildings, they were told that they were not allowed to photograph "light rail, bus stops, bank buildings, stadiums, street lights, or the airport." Although they were not arrested, they were questioned for some time and generally treated poorly by the officer. Even when they were through being interrogated, the officer left and said that he would be watching them to make sure they didn't take illegal pictures.

At no time were these men provided with information regarding which statute they were violating. They were not provided with this information because, technically, it's not illegal. The conclusion here is that the police officer himself was confused about the law. Rather than admitting he was wrong, or calling to ask for help, he told the men to "google it" when they asked which statute they were violating. This might not happen if we had fewer laws. Police in Long Beach have confirmed that it is within their departmental policy to detain photographers if their subject has no aesthetic value[45]. This purely subjective quality is, of course, up

---

44 http://downtownphoenixjournal.com/2009/04/02/photography-crime-phoenix/

45 http://www.lbpost.com/life/greggory/12188

to them to determine, not the photographer. While it's not, technically, illegal, it might as well be if it results in that kind of treatment by those who are supposed to *protect and serve* us.

In case you started to feel some relief that photography is still legal, don't decompress just yet. A man in Tennessee was questioned and actually arrested for unlawful photography[46]. His supposed crime was taking a picture of a law enforcement officer. The officer told him that it was illegal.

Later, the officer said he thought that the man was pointing a laser at him. However, the iPhone that took the picture didn't have a flash or even a light that could be mistaken for a laser. It turns out that it's not illegal to photograph an officer on a public highway in Tennessee, either. This officer was confused, too.

Maybe the officers are simply mistaken. Maybe they just have too many laws to keep track of. Or maybe they want to be the only ones able to take pictures. I had to pay a ticket because of a picture taken by a traffic signal camera a few years ago, and I'm still upset about it. I wonder how long that stays on file. I'm thinking about requesting a copy of that photo to put in a scrapbook some day.

Maybe the last two examples of supposed illegal photography don't hit home with you. I suppose most people

---

46 http://www2.tricities.com/news/2008/jul/12/man_arrested_for_unlawful_photography-ar-254606/

aren't taking outdoor architectural pictures or asking officers to smile for the camera. Maybe you're the type who doesn't like to stir controversy. Maybe you just want to take your camera to the park on a nice day and photograph your children playing with their friends. Please be careful, though. That can be illegal, too.

A man in Idaho was recently labeled as suspicious for photographing children at a local park[47]. He left when a woman started yelling at him. She called the police and they were on the lookout for a suspicious person with a camera. I guess they were worried about pedophilia. But, it turns out that the guy was just taking pictures of his grandson and left when the woman was harassing him.

Two photographers were taking pictures of kids running in sprinklers at a public park in Boston when they were told it wasn't allowed[48]. The photographer admits to enjoying photographing kids, but before you think the worst, he likes it because "they are so natural in front of the camera." Here is an artist that wants to capture the innocence and abandon of youth and is automatically labeled as deviant.

It might be determined that this person wasn't breaking the law, but it might be better to spend the night in jail than to be

---

47 http://www.pixiq.com/article/man-photographing-grandkid-in-park-deemed-suspicious

48 http://www.pixiq.com/article/photogs-told-not-allowed-to-photograph-kids-in-public-park

unjustifiably labeled as a pedophile. Is there a worse stigma in our society? While it is normally only illegal in the court of public opinion to photograph kids, New Jersey is actually considering making it an official crime[49].

One of my favorite and most cherished books is a book of photographs called "All Smiles" by Bruce Velick. My college photography professor gave me this book as a get well present when I was in an accident. The book contains pictures of people smiling. It was (and is) therapeutic to me.

None of the pictures seem staged. I have my doubts about whether Mr. Velick obtained permission slips from parents before snapping some of the most joyful photographs I've ever seen.

There are toothless kids running toward the camera and the mischievous faces of a little league team. There are shirtless boys making playful gestures and a proud little one holding a package to deliver. There's the image of a girl enduring a vaccination while her friends look on and laugh nervously while they wait their turn. The photographer managed to capture the essence of youth. Kids are depicted running through the sprinkler, dancing, clapping, playing hopscotch, and nursing. Like I said, I cherish this book and these pictures. I just hope the wrong person isn't reading these words. Someone might confiscate my beloved

---

[49] http://www.nydailynews.com/news/national/2011/05/09/2011-05-09_new_jersey_considers_bill_that_would_ban_photographing_children_lawmakers_weigh_.html

book and label it as child pornography somehow. Worse yet, great pictures like these might never be taken again if laws like this get passed.

Maybe I'm getting too sentimental. I'll focus on something more concrete for a minute. Have you ever taken a picture of your own child in the bath? Most people with kids have. It's a neat thing to document – their behavior in the bath as youngsters or their terrified faces during their first bath. But, be warned, your life could change forever if the wrong person finds out.

One man who took his kids camping made the mistake of his life – getting his family pictures processed the old-fashioned way. When several pictures he took of swimming and other camping-related activities were developed at a store, he was turned in for child pornography[50].

He was eventually cleared of all charges, but see in his own words how the traumatic experience affected his life:

> *...my wife and I, our children and friends, lived in a kind of suspended animation, a limbo of unreality where our privacy was invaded and we were stripped of our sense of dignity and seemingly our rights. To be accused unjustly of any crime is a terrible thing. But to be accused of using your own children for pornographic purposes or sexual exploitation bears a special taint because no matter how*

---

50 http://www.salon.com/life/feature/2006/07/18/photos

highly people think of you, they don't know you in your most intimate moments, which forever leaves you open to suspicion.

I couldn't say it any better. And, I don't think it's very different at all from taking a picture of your kid in the bath. For this man, it resulted in a drawn out case with family services and the constant threat of taking his children away.

Conclusion

As the scientific method would dictate, every experiment must end with a conclusion. While this experiment on my friends isn't exactly objective, there are some conclusions that can be drawn.

First of all, my friends had better be careful. If the wrong person overheard their conversations about such egregious criminal activities, they could be the next ones making big news being hauled off to jail.

In all seriousness, one of the conclusions I take from this little experiment on my friends is that far more things that used to be considered benign are gathering steam as criminal offenses. The sad reality is that many people with no previous criminal record are being charged and punished as criminals for normal behaviors that many of us wouldn't think twice about.

I don't know how they feel about being my lab rats, but I consider the experiment on my friends a success. Topics that they naturally brought up could easily be turned into conversations about breaking the law, and they're not talking about selling drugs or attempted murder. They're talking about gardens, school, and rummage sales. So maybe Jack Handey really was onto something when he said that any conversation could be turned into a discussion about breaking the law.

I suppose my experiment would have been more scientifically valid if I actually reported numbers. But, it also would have been more annoying and the last thing I want to do is annoy somebody because it's probably against the law, and I'm trying to follow the rules here.

After examining my friends, I find myself more and more curious about whether I am following the law. I'm trying to follow the rules, but there's only one way to find out whether I'm succeeding or not – I need to take my turn in the maze.

MY TURN IN THE MAZE

I don't remember the setting, but I once heard that only criminals need to know the laws. The assumption is that a deviant person will want to know the letter of the law in order to get as close to the edge as possible while still remaining within the legal bounds. This theory also assumes that decent people will automatically follow the laws of the land simply by being decent people. I used to believe this.

Maybe you believe this, too. If so, it's because the media reinforces it. You've probably seen a TV show (reality or otherwise) where the following scenario is played out: A person has been arrested for something. They object to their arrest and mildly resist. Before long, they are being dragged into the police car in handcuffs while yelling about their rights. For most people, the natural reaction is probably to cheer the police for getting another criminal off the streets and to assume that the handcuffed individual doesn't have a leg to stand on. These assumptions reinforce the false ideas that everyone who is arrested is guilty and that only criminals know their rights.

We assume that criminals don't have any rights or if they do, they shouldn't. Speaking about criminals and their rights conjures up images of county jails with bercaloungers and cable television. I've found myself having those thoughts before.

If the majority of people continue to have these false assumptions, common citizens will be hauled off on a regular basis for violations like those discussed in the last chapter. With the assumption that we all need to know the laws and since I've always heard that ignorance is no excuse, I decided to do another experiment.

This time, instead of eavesdropping on my friends' conversations, I am going to test myself. My turn in the maze involves me reading all of the municipal codes in my city (yawn) to see if I am following them. I will also ponder and discuss reasonable hypothetical situations that could arise in my life as they relate to the codes. If I find that I am violating any codes, I will attempt to rectify that situation as part of this ongoing experiment in following the rules.

I live in Marion, Indiana, but this could be the story of any small- to medium-sized community in America. Nothing I write here is meant as a political jab against the mayor, city council, or anyone else in charge. I don't know those people and don't have a beef with any of them. I enjoy living here. It is my home, and I plan to stay for a while.

Securing a copy of the codes was my first order of business. They are available to read online, but I wanted to be able to print them off to make notes and markings. There is an option to print the codes, but the page that loads contains only nonsensical characters, even when viewing the page using several different web browsers.

I emailed one of the four code enforcement officers in order to ask if paper copies were available. I never heard back from him. Since I wanted to avoid strange stares and glances when asking for a copy of the codes in person, I decided to copy and paste them from the internet into a new document. This required clicking on individual ordinances, copying them, and pasting them since you can't see the whole document at once. Despite the inconvenience, things were going along well until I read the following disclaimer (emphasis added):

> *This Code of Ordinances and/or any other documents that appear on this site may not reflect the most current legislation adopted by the Municipality.*

> *American Legal Publishing Corporation provides these documents for informational purposes only. These documents should not be relied upon as the definitive authority for local legislation. Additionally, the formatting and pagination of the posted documents varies from the formatting and pagination of the official copy.* **The official printed copy of a Code of Ordinances should be consulted prior to any action being taken**[51].

At that point, I determined it would be best to make sure that I was working with the most up-to-date information. For an undertaking like this, it would probably be best to consult the "official printed copy."

I made my way to the municipal building downtown. In a way, I could not believe I was doing this. Being the type of person who doesn't like to make waves, I was prepared for all kinds of questions. I was thinking they would take my fingerprints, ask to see my social security card and a picture identification, and want to know my intent behind wanting a copy of the codes.

The actual incident was unremarkable except for the fact that I didn't come away with a copy of the codes in hand. It turns out that no "official printed copy" exists. After asking at two desks, a lady came out with a rather large binder to show me the codes.

---

51 http://www.amlegal.com/nxt/gateway.dll/Indiana/marion_in/marionindiana?f=templates$fn=default.htm$3.0$vid=amlegal:marion_in

She said the ones she had there were last codified in 2005, they would cost a fortune to copy, and they were already out of date. She was right. The online municipal codes have a date of 2006 on them. They're probably out of date, too, but, they're the best thing available. Therefore, I'm going with it, even though the disclaimer warned not to rely on it as the "definitive authority for local legislation." The fact is I have no other choice.

I finished my copying and pasting routine until I had 296 pages, even after reducing the font size and not including headings. After realizing it would take several ink cartridges to print these, I decided to get them printed at a local store even though more weird looks would undoubtedly come my way. It turns out the woman at the municipal building was correct on another count – they did cost a fortune to copy. And the process took a significant portion of my morning. The final product was immense – too large for one binding, in fact.

Simply looking at the mound of papers in front of me was daunting and led me to believe that there is little chance that any other resident in this town's history has ever done what I just did. It is therefore reasonable to question whether any other common citizen (or elected official) has ever read all of the municipal codes.

At a quick glance, I can tell that the language doesn't use common vernacular and is confusing to just about anyone on my side of law school. If regular people can't understand these codes, then they are most likely violating many of them. Of course, there's little way of knowing this other than trying to make sense of them yourself.

The city seems to recognize that the information needs to be disseminated to the public in a form they can digest. In small doses on the website, residents are made aware of the most common code violations. This section lists only six items and four of them have to do with garbage. If you want to know about any other topics, you need to pull a Sherlock Holmes and investigate them for yourself. Otherwise, don't be surprised if a code enforcement officer stops by your residence to inform you of a violation you are committing.

The codes in my town contain the following categories, some of which will be more applicable to me than others: general provisions, administration, public works, traffic code, general regulations, business regulations, general offenses, and land usage. As I reference the codes throughout this chapter, they will be listed in direct quotes with no other reference given since it will not be relevant to most readers.

A quick review of the scientific method will guide us through this chapter. First, I spent the previous chapter reporting on some *observations* that I have been making lately. My *question* is whether I am the law-abiding citizen that I thought I was. I *hypothesize* (based on the last chapter's observations) that I am not qualified to make that statement. My *experiment* is to read all of my city's municipal codes and decide whether I am truly the upright citizen that I always thought I was. Discussion and *conclusions* will follow.

One of the first things I read was in the *general provisions* section. It was giving an example of a code later in the book. It reads "This municipality shall make available to any person for inspection or copying all public records, unless otherwise exempted by state law." I specifically went in to the municipal building to get a copy of these codes and couldn't do it. Either I wasn't insistent enough or they're ignoring their own regulations because I would think that the municipal codes would be part of the "public record." Simply having the codes on the internet is not good enough because not everyone has access to this medium.

While I am truly amazed by how many municipal codes exist in my sleepy little town, I do have to admit that most of them do not relate to me or my everyday life. Among other fascinating topics, I've read a lot about cross connection control devices (I still don't know what they are), maintenance of water meter boxes, and the city civil defense organization.

I'd be willing to bet that most of the people discussed in the last chapter thought that the city codes didn't apply to them, either. As I have already delineated, such an assumption can land a person in hot water. So, I am determined to press on, follow all of the rules, and find out how it feels when the codes and regulations do hit close to home. It didn't take long to find out.

Regarding Garbage

Garbage collection seems to be a popular topic in municipal codes. This is not surprising since a city's efficiency at removing solid waste contributes heavily to the image the city portrays. It is understandable that the city has guidelines and procedures in place regarding this topic. We will soon find out how reasonable these guidelines and procedures are for the average person like myself.

In the residential waste procedures section, I found a number of regulations that I'm certain I have violated. First of all, before throwing it away or recycling it, the code indicates that "all broken glass shall be wrapped." It doesn't say what type of wrapping a person should use, but just that it should be wrapped. I'm sure I've broken a light bulb or two and just thrown them away or recycled the glass pieces. From now on, I'll be sure to wrap them in something – Christmas wrapping paper, perhaps?

What happens, though, if the glass I break happens to be a compact fluorescent light (CFL) bulb? Then, I will not just be violating a municipal code; I will be polluting the environment. One of the biggest troubles I see with giant stacks of legislation is that the laws and regulations end up canceling each other out or making something more confusing than it needs to be. The pertinent example here is the fact that, thanks to our government, we will soon be unable to purchase incandescent light bulbs at the store. The most popular replacement is the CFL[52].

The Energy Independence and Security Act of 2007[53] will be responsible for the death of the incandescent light bulb. Besides being sentimental about losing one of Edison's finest inventions, I am concerned about other ramifications associated with this change – specifically the fact that there is debate as to whether their net benefits to the environment are significant enough to snuff out personal choice in the matter.

Here is where government gets in the way. The mandated new bulbs, while being more efficient, are a public health concern. For starters, they contain mercury. The Environmental Protection Agency (EPA) indicates that mercury exposure can cause the following[54]:

- Impaired neurological development
- Impaired peripheral vision
- Disturbances in sensations
- Muscle weakness

---

52 http://en.wikipedia.org/wiki/Phase-out_of_incandescent_light_bulbs
53 http://thomas.loc.gov/cgi-bin/bdquery/z?d110:H.R.6:
54 http://www.epa.gov/mercury/effects.htm

- Lack of coordination of movements
- Impairment of speech and hearing

In addition to these, there is some evidence that mercury exposure can cause cancer. The EPA doesn't confirm this, but admits that there is not enough data. They do acknowledge, however, that exposure to mercury has been linked to tumor formation in rats and mice.

Even my little municipality knows that mercury is dangerous and has written a prohibition against putting too much of it into waste-water. So, what are we supposed to do with our CFLs?

According to the EPA, we should recycle all burned out CFLs[55]. If this is not possible, they recommend sealing the bulb in a plastic bag and treating it like normal trash "if your state or local environmental regulatory agency permits." I would expect more than ninety-eight percent of people aren't going to double-check that. They won't do as much research as I just did. They'll just toss it into the trash and inadvertently put mercury into landfills, where it will more than likely infiltrate and contaminate groundwater[56]. If a CFL bulb breaks before it is disposed, there is a

---

55 http://www.epa.gov/cfl/cflrecycling.html

56 http://www.greenmuze.com/blogs/guest-bloggers/1031-the-dark-side-of-cfls.html

more detailed procedure in place. It includes the following precautions[57]:

- Having people leave the room
- Having pets leave the room
- Airing out the room
- Shutting off heating or air conditioning systems
- Using duct tape to pick up all small glass fragments and powder (vacuuming is not recommended until after this step is complete since it can spread mercury vapors)

These EPA guidelines certainly seem to imply that CFLs are dangerous. You would never see precautions to this extent for a broken incandescent light bulb. If this sounds like a burden, get used to it or get used to breaking the rules. A person who is trying to follow all of the rules will, on one hand be told that they can't dispose of mercury and, on the other hand be forced to buy products containing it.

I have heard it said that the traditional incandescent light bulb is responsible for releasing more mercury into the environment over the course of its lifetime than a CFL because of the coal-burning process used for most electricity-generating power plants. While this may be true, there probably isn't any way of knowing for sure since it depends on many factors, such as the

---

57 http://epa.gov/cfl/cflcleanup-detailed.html

origin and quality of the coal used in coal-burning plants (the amount of recoverable mercury in coal differs by region). In addition, this argument would not hold up if the electricity came from power plants that don't use fossil fuels. For example, wind- or solar panel-driven electricity generation, both of which are becoming increasingly popular, would obviously release no mercury into the atmosphere.

While this is an interesting debate, I am not sure if exact numbers can be known. Remember that CFLs, while more energy-efficient, are still powered by the same mercury-emitting power plants; but in addition they also contain mercury collected specifically for their manufacture. In either case, The United States Department of Energy indicates that coal-fired power plants contribute less than 1% of the total amount of mercury emitted globally[58].

Even if CFLs result in a net gain for the environment in terms of mercury emissions, there are still other environmental factors to consider – namely that all CFLs are imported. They say that if every house in America installed just one CFL, it would be equivalent to taking "7.5 million cars off the road"[59]. But, the use of

---

58 http://www.fossil.energy.gov/programs/powersystems/pollutioncontrols/overview_mercurycontrols.html

59 http://environment.about.com/od/greenlivingdesign/a/light_bulbs.htm

CFLs in America also puts vehicles on the road, boats in the water, and planes in the air just to get them here[60].

At this point, the discussion really revolves around personal freedom of choice for lighting. I've seen amusing shirts and bumper stickers announcing, "I'm pro-choice," with a picture of a light bulb. The fact remains that CFLs are not a clear-cut choice for environmentally conscious consumers. Even environmental websites point out a variety of health concerns associated with CFL use. The following quote is by Dr. Magda Havas, associate professor of environmental and resource studies, Trent University Peterborough, Ontario, Canada regarding harmful ultraviolet radiation[61]:

> *Tube fluorescent bulbs have diffusers that filter the UV radiation. Compact fluorescent light bulbs do not have these diffusers, and hence people using CFLs are exposed to UV radiation. UV radiation has been linked to skin cancer and various skin disorders. Those who have skin problems may be particularly sensitive to this radiation.*

As usual, more studies need to be done and more information needs to be gathered before we'll know enough about how CFLs are truly affecting the environment. But, the

---

60 http://peswiki.com/index.php/Directory:Compact_Fluorescent_Lighting_%28CFL%29_Downsides

61 http://www.renewableenergygeek.ca/energy-efficiency/cfls-emit-ultraviolet-radiation-energy-efficient-light-bulbs-unscrewed-part-2/

government doesn't bother to gather that information before banning the old standby. Either way, I won't be throwing my light bulbs away without wrapping them from now on.

The next garbage-related code that I'm certain I've violated is the fact that I cannot have more than two receptacles out for collection per week without a city sanitation label. Prior to reading these codes, I wasn't even aware that a city sanitation label existed. Apparently, you can purchase them "from the city or its duly authorized and designated retail agents at a cost of $1 per label."

Typically, we don't produce a lot of garbage at our house. Often, we don't even have to put out the garbage every week since the bulk of it gets recycled. But, it has happened a time or two that we had more than two receptacles out for collection – when we moved in, after having a lot of company, and after grandparents spoiled my kids with tons of birthday presents. Maybe I'm a masochist, but I'm kind of looking forward to trying to follow this rule the next time it comes up. If obtaining these city sanitation labels is anything like trying to obtain a copy of the municipal codes, I'm in for a good laugh.

My little city hasn't caught up with some forward-thinking communities in terms of garbage collection restrictions. Even though my trash impact is relatively small, I would be in big trouble in San Francisco. They are trying to go to a zero waste program by 2020[62]. As part of this effort, recycling and composting are mandatory.

Composting is a great way to reduce municipal solid waste while also improving the environment. The trouble is, government officials can't seem to make up their minds about it. On one hand, San Francisco is encouraging composting and even passing out approved bins for collection purposes. But other cities in California are telling residents to "cease and desist" composting[63].

In 2008, a woman was asked to stop composting without a solid waste permit because she was collecting compostable materials from a local restaurant. She was taking things that would have otherwise been thrown into a landfill and turned them into nutrient-rich soil for her plants. This dually beneficial practice was halted through the typical avenue – a complaint by a neighbor.

If I put myself in the shoes of the woman who was composting illegally, I can imagine I'd be pretty upset. Here we have a situation where she has probably been encouraged to compost for environmental reasons and then told she has to stop because someone is annoyed. For the record, her compost was stored in wooden boxes covered with black plastic.

When I consider the other viewpoint, I can't say I can blame the neighbors for complaining. I don't really know how I'd

---

62 http://www.sfenvironment.org/our_programs/overview.html?ssi=3
63 http://articles.latimes.com/2008/dec/26/local/me-compost26

feel if my neighbors started gathering food scraps from dumpsters and collecting it in a pile in their yard. My point is that we need to get it together and give one, consistent message before the majority of us give up trying to follow the rules at all. In the meantime, some of my neighbors would do well to read this:

> *Residential waste scattered by animals or weather shall be removed promptly by the owner or occupant of the dwelling unit. The owner or occupant of the dwelling unit shall promptly remove scattered or strewn waste resulting from broken, damaged or overturned receptacles.*

I might give up recycling if they are serious about the next code I read about. The code states that I must "rinse, drain and segregate" all of my recyclables. I do rinse and drain them, but I do not segregate them. The city only gives one bin for all of the recycling. With this method of collection, they can't really expect segregation. Until I read this, I didn't even know it was expected since it's certainly not implied from the manner in which it is collected – all recyclables get thrown into a big pile in a single truck. I don't know anyone in town that segregates their recyclables.

Nevertheless, for the purpose of this experiment, I attempted to segregate my recyclables. I separated everything out and put each type of recyclable in its own sack. Each sack was then placed in the large receptacle that the city provides.

Then, for research purposes, I snooped in my neighbors' curbside recycling bins. My worst fears were confirmed – I am living alongside anarchists. None of the bins I saw had anything segregated.

Moreover, several of the bins were out before 7:00 p.m. on the night before collection. This is another ordinance of which I just became aware. "All receptacles shall be placed on the collection site no earlier than 7:00 p.m. on the day preceding the scheduled collection." For my purposes, I am glad that my neighbors violated this code. Otherwise, I would have looked very suspicious peering into their recycling bins as I walked down the street in the dark.

My neighbors routinely have their garbage and recycling out at the curb prior to 7:00 p.m. the night before collection. Sometimes I do, too. Typically, I see their recyclables outside, and that is what reminds me to put mine out. However, this is a violation of the municipal code. Thank goodness for the conscientious objectors that remind the rest of us slackers to get in gear.

Speaking of slackers, "all receptacles shall be removed from their collection site on the same day as the collection is made." Guilty as charged. The problem here is that I don't read any exception to the rule for pregnancy or simple laziness. For all I know, it has probably even happened in my household that I have taken the garbage out to the cans that are still on the curb from the previous collection. Maybe they don't notice it because I have collection via the back alley rather than the street. Anyway, it won't happen again. I'm going to follow the rules from now on.

As far as I can tell, that's the end to my violations of the city's garbage-related ordinances. It's time to move on to something more serious.

Traffic Violations

In my town, you can only cross the street at a 90-degree angle unless the crosswalk dictates it. Maybe they should have just told people to remain in the crosswalks. Instead, they said, "No pedestrian shall cross a roadway at any place other than by a route at right angles to the curb or by the shortest route to the opposite curb except in a crosswalk." Also, "between adjacent intersections at which official traffic-control signals are in operation, pedestrians shall not cross at any place except in a crosswalk."

As I take my late summer strolls this year, I'll be sure to stay within the crosswalks. I am sure that I violate this rule on a regular basis. I always thought that jaywalking was a joke. It's one of those things that I've always been told is, technically, illegal, but I wasn't so sure I believed it until now.

In my short time on this planet, I have seen jaywalking occur approximately 1.4 million times. I have never witnessed anyone getting a ticket for it, and I live on a busy street. In my opinion it is far more dangerous and annoying to encounter someone practicing *jaybiking*. Jaywalking is for the novice code violator.

It turns out, I am in violation of more than one ordinance when I jaywalk. I usually have my stroller with me and at least one child. If I happen to jaywalk with my child, I could get two fines. Technically, if I happen to jaywalk with both of my kids in the double stroller, I could get three fines. "The parent of any child and the guardian of any ward shall not authorize or knowingly permit any such child or ward to violate any of the provisions of this chapter." Good thing I plan to follow the rules because otherwise these fines would be racking up. I wonder if the city knows about this vast, untapped source of revenue.

I see pedestrians every day as I sit in my home office. Quite a few do not use crosswalks, and even if they do, they sometimes proceed at what I would estimate to be about a 75-degree angle, rather than a 90. What is the world coming to?

Fire Hazards

In my town, we are allowed to burn yard waste. We bought a 55-gallon drum from a guy's yard outside of town for $12. Sometimes visitors see our barrel in the backyard and comment that they're surprised that we are allowed to burn our garbage here. To clarify, we aren't burning garbage, and technically, I don't think that is allowed.

Once in a while the stars align just right, and my husband decides to do some yard work other than mowing. He trims our hedges and trees, rakes up the clippings, and burns them in the barrel. Even though this is allowed in my town, we're still managing to break the law on several fronts.

First of all, the code states:

> *No person shall burn combustible materials except between the hours of 6:00 a.m. and 6:00 p.m. No fire shall be permitted to burn, smolder or smoke after 6:00 p.m. and shall be totally extinguished at 7:00 p.m.*

For us, 6:00 p.m. comes pretty early, especially in the summer. For us to follow this ordinance, we can only burn on weekends because my husband doesn't even return from work until 6:00 p.m. I think most of our fires have been *started* at that time rather than ended. According to the city, we're all backward on our times. We have our garbage out too early and our fires going too late.

The second manner in which we are violating the burning regulations is by not having a mesh cover on our barrel. All materials must be burned in an *adequate container*. This is defined as a "non-combustible 55-gallon barrel or drum sufficiently vented to induce adequate primary combustion air with enclosed sides, a bottom and a mesh covering with openings no larger than 1/4" square."

Our barrel is 55 gallons. Our barrel is sufficiently vented. Our barrel has sides and a bottom. But, we lack the mesh cover. A lot of outdoor fireplaces have mesh covers, but I have never seen one for a burning barrel. Our next burning will probably occur in the fall, but I need to be in compliance by then. Read about my quest to obtain the proper cover for my burning barrel in Field Journal A.

Noise Violations

I planned to breeze through the noise violation section in the municipal codes. Other than possessing a boisterous laugh, I'm not known for being especially loud. Even my children are used to it being quiet and tend to get overwhelmed when we have company.

I get annoyed at loud music, partying, and especially hearing other people's arguments. I like things to be peaceful and quiet. But, I do own a motorcycle and so does my husband. Mine isn't especially loud even though we've changed mufflers from the stock Suzuki pipe to a stock Harley-Davidson pipe. But, my husband's motorcycle is definitely illegal according to the municipal codes.

I would have said that it was *probably* illegal, but I went out and bought a decibel meter to find out for sure. See Field Journal B for the lab report on this experiment. The code is actually specific enough to delineate exactly how much noise you can make. If a vehicle produces over 80 decibels within the city, it's illegal. It actually gets more specific than that. The code reads:

> *No person shall cause the sound pressure level of the noise emitted during the operation of a light motor vehicle to exceed 80 DBA in speed zones of 45 miles per hour or less within the city. The sound pressure level measurement shall be made at a distance of not less than 15 feet from the edge of the lane of travel of the violator.*

I wanted to know if it was just me, or if other people were violating the noise ordinance as well. See Field Journal C for the full report. The report doesn't mention it, but I witnessed about as many jaywalkers during this time as noise violators.

After all of that experimentation, the point here isn't whether we're over the limit or not with our motorcycle or how many others are violating the ordinance. The point is that there's no way for a regular person to quickly and easily know whether they are in violation or not. Besides the fact that the ordinances are difficult to obtain and understand, they are too specific to allow a regular person to reasonably attempt to follow them.

Truthfully, I don't know how to obey this ordinance on a regular basis. I don't think I can convince my husband to buy new pipes for his motorcycle. Maybe the best thing to do is ride the motorcycle straight out of town, which is what he usually does.

Pet Violations

I was really relieved to find out that I am not the only member of my household that is violating ordinances without knowing it – my cats are also in violation. They have been vaccinated against rabies, but they do not wear the rabies vaccination tag "at all times." I recently obtained the tags, but the cats aren't wearing them because they're fairly bulky and, I'm guessing, would be uncomfortable. The good news is that my cats aren't going to tell on me.

Pets are also supposed to be registered with the city. This is supposed to be done every year at a cost of $2 each. Since I have two cats, this would amount to $4 per year. The fine for violating this ordinance, however, is much more significant.

> *Persons violating this section shall be subject to a fine in the amount of $50. Each day of noncompliance shall constitute a separate violation. In addition to the fine, an unlicensed animal is subject to impound by the Animal Control Service until proper licensing is obtained.*

I've lived here for about 13 months now. At $50 per day, the charge for leaving my cats unregistered is pretty significant. The worst part would be having them confiscated, though. This is unacceptable, so I attempted to register my cats. You can read about my quest to register my cats in Field Journal D.

One of my cats is an outdoor cat. Several years ago he forgot how to behave indoors. Specifically, he forgot proper bathroom procedures. I tried everything to fix his poor behavior and to clean up after him. I bought another litter box. I moved his food far away from the litter box. I spent too much money on cleaners and a steam vacuum. I even put diapers on the cat after watching a video on the internet about it. Finally, I bought a large and quite expensive outdoor cage for him.

In the cold winter months and during bad weather, he spends time in our breezeway, a concrete-floored room that joins our house to the garage. The rest of the time is spent in his outdoor cage. It's big enough to house several cats, and it even has tunnels for him to explore. He likes it, but it doesn't allow much freedom. Therefore, I sometimes put him on a long leash, which lets him roam around in the backyard and explore beyond the cage.

I didn't know until recently that I could only have him on the leash a certain amount of time per day. Sometimes he spends several hours on the leash. But, the city code clearly states "no animal will be tethered for more than three hours during any 24-hour period." To me, that seems extreme since the leash actually allows a bit more freedom than the cage. But, in order to follow the rules, I need to cage my cat, rather than tether him.

Conclusion

At the beginning of this chapter I hypothesized that I was not qualified to make the statement that I am a law-abiding citizen. Although I've tried my best to be in compliance with the codes, I still find myself in violation on several fronts. I believe the experiments in this chapter, which are documented in the field journals, serve to prove my hypothesis correct.

Both this chapter and the previous one have pointed out several ways in which we are given mixed messages from the government at all levels. More contradictions come your way in the upcoming chapters. It's no wonder some people have given up trying to comply. It's hard to know what to do when we're told to *think globally and act locally*, but we're not allowed to sell vegetables to passers-by or buy light bulbs made in this country.

My time in the maze has been tough. The previous chapter's investigations were much easier. For me to have to read the codes and attempt to follow them has been much more of a hassle than I thought. Just sorting my recycling slowed down my weekly routine by at least 15 minutes. When I found out that my cats had to be registered, I thought twice about attempting to follow the rules. I really didn't want to be bothered with trying to follow rules that never get enforced and don't seem to matter to anyone.

    This exposé of my personal life has come to a close. Now everyone knows which city ordinances I am violating, and I have no excuse not to comply. In fact, I am motivated more than ever to comply since I just spent the last chapter telling on myself.

FIELD OBSERVATION

Every day that it is in session, Congress discusses new legislation. Sometimes this takes place on the floor, and sometimes in committees. Sometimes you can even see it on C-span. Many of the things they discuss will never become public law, but some of it will.

So far, about two dozen house resolutions have been signed into public law during the current congress (112th). Approximately one quarter of them have been focused on naming a building after someone. I am sure that W. Craig Broadwater's family is very thankful for the great honor of the Federal building and United States courthouse in Martinsburg, West Virginia bearing his name[64]. I'm also pretty sure that nobody else cares all that much other than Mr. Jay Rockefeller, the senior United States Senator from West Virginia who introduced the bill[65].

Once in a while, however, something Congress does makes us stand up and pay attention. A few years ago we were focused on the big health bill, *Obamacare*, as it has now been labeled. More recently, we were focused on the debt ceiling discussions. But, usually, we're not paying any attention because most of the stuff that occurs doesn't affect us in a meaningful way.

Only when something happens to our neighbors, our family, or ourselves are most of us jolted into having an opinion on legal matters. I've discussed throughout this book how people throughout the United States are regularly breaking laws that they didn't even know existed. I have proven that any reasonable person can find him- or herself in the uncomfortable position of dealing with a law enforcement officer by giving examples from every day conversations and my own life.

But, there is some unfinished business. The things I am about to discuss might not be things my friends are talking about or things that my city's municipal code addresses, but they are issues that I see as equally important in this context. I will focus this chapter on giving more details about some of the problems

---

[64] http://thomas.loc.gov/cgi-bin/bdquery/D?d112:16:./temp/~bdP5st::|/bss/d112query.html|
[65] http://en.wikipedia.org/wiki/John_D._Rockefeller_IV

that I set forth in the first chapter, specifically those that were not already discussed at length.

Selective Enforcement

Generally speaking, municipal codes are not enforced. If they were, I would already have been aware of the codes that I was violating without needing to endure the agony of reading all of them. The very first time I set out more than two receptacles of trash without a city sanitation label, I would have been issued a citation.

Since they are not enforced regularly, we can only assume they are enforced selectively. A number of factors probably contribute to a person receiving a trash-related violation. It's possible that the person puts out dozens of trash receptacles each week and the garbage collectors are tired of dealing with it. Or maybe they live in a really nice part of town that is more heavily monitored. But, I suspect the difference in the person who is ticketed and the person who isn't is simply a matter of neighbors.

Selective enforcement of rules leads to tit-for-tat between neighbors. I suspect that neighbors are responsible for turning in most people who are ticketed for trash-related offenses (and other codes that are selectively enforced). Along those lines, I suspect that most people don't actually have a problem with the amount of trash their neighbors produce. More than likely, something else ticked them off and they choose to get the law involved to get even.

When code enforcement officers ticket someone for not obeying the letter of the law, they could probably go down the street and find numerous other violations. But, they choose to ticket the individuals that they do in order to satisfy the complaining party. It probably comes as no surprise to officers when they soon get a report concerning a code violation at the original complaining party's residence.

Selective enforcement also allows individuals to be punished for unrelated and noncriminal social behaviors. For example, selective enforcement could be used against the coach who cut someone's son from the baseball team or the jury member that found someone guilty. By reporting these people for minor municipal code violations, they are, in effect, being punished for other matters. It could go on forever that way.

I grew up in the country. We didn't have close neighbors. I don't know first-hand, but people tell me that, as a society, we aren't as neighborly as we used to be. They say that a positive sense of community is lost in our cities and villages. If that's true, I'm sure law enforcement officers are tired of attempting to settle our differences using legal means. We should be tired of it, too.

I suspect one reason that municipal codes are not enforced is because the municipality isn't doing their job, either. It would be pretty hypocritical for city officials to issue citations for public nuisances such as tall weeds or junk cars when they have to trip over crumbling streets to get to the violator's residence.

If codes were enforced equally across the board, there would be more justice in our society. I wouldn't be able to look down the street at my neighbor's six-month-old leftover rummage sale and wonder if that would be allowed on the north side of town. I don't know if consistency is possible, but we can definitely do better.

Unenforceable Regulations

A few times a year, a city I used to live in published a circular containing an interesting section: City Ordinances to Know. This little flier taught me about low-hanging branches over sidewalks, noise regulations, and trash collection practices. It also taught me that there is no way of enforcing most of the city ordinances. I suppose the bulletin was a last-ditch effort to inform us of regulations in the hope that we would comply just because we know the rules.

One thing I learned was that a person cannot have their car parked on any city street for more than two consecutive days. I'd like to know how they would go about enforcing that. As far as I can tell, they would have to set up surveillance on the vehicle or rely on the testimony of neighbors, which is dicey at best and leads to issues of selective enforcement.

I doubt anyone has ever been cited for this violation. First of all, a neighbor's testimony is not necessarily reliable and secondly, the city probably will not bother to put a plainclothes officer on the lookout for stationary cars for two whole days. Without issuing a citation, the city probably can't expect compliance simply by distributing a newsletter. I know the newsletter didn't motivate my neighbors to move their old truck. It stayed in the same spot along the street for almost two years.

Vague Codes

Laws that are vague are meaningless. Worse yet, they can be spiteful and only addressed because of someone's pet peeve. In chapter two I gave the example of a woman not allowed to grow vegetables in her front yard because it wasn't considered a *suitable* place for a garden. It doesn't take a genius to figure out that what is suitable for one person might not be suitable for another.

In some communities, it is illegal to dry your clothes outside on a clothesline[66]. Clotheslines are illegal in communities that prioritize appearance over common sense. Some laws in this country are in place to protect the environment, as the case with the CFL vs. incandescent bulbs demonstrates, while others force us to harm the environment through electricity use. Electric clothes dryers account for up to 6% of our nation's energy use.

---
66 http://www.latimes.com/features/la-hm-clothesline7-2009feb07,0,6872149.story

Wouldn't it make sense to cut down on that by hanging clothes outside? No, because that can be construed as a *public nuisance* or *unsuitable* in many communities' vague ordinances. You see, in this day and age hanging clothes out on a line is associated with the poor, and some communities have higher standards[67]. If you want to save energy in those communities, you have to buy a Toyota Prius. That's the fashionable thing to do.

If laws aren't specific enough, the problem of selective enforcement begins to play a factor. What is suitable for me might not be suitable to the code enforcement officer or vice versa. To me, it is not suitable for a person to mow their lawn in their underwear, but some people don't have a problem with it. I suspect, however, that those who may not object probably have nice looking neighbors.

Perhaps the codes need to be more specific, but then we run into a different set of problems.

Ultra-Specific Codes

In chapter three, I discussed the specific nature of the noise ordinances in my city. The code was specific enough to list legal and illegal levels of noise by decibel even though these numbers are meaningless to a person without a decibel meter.

---

[67] http://www.ajc.com/opinion/content/opinion/stories/2008/08/05/homeownersed_0806.html

Blood alcohol levels pose a similar problem. Of course I don't agree with driving while intoxicated, but does anyone who drinks and drives actually know whether they're over the legal blood alcohol limit? Not unless they have a personal breathalyzer. If a common citizen can't readily determine whether he or she is breaking a particular law, then that law is flawed. People are left to take their best guess as to whether they are within the legal limits, and that is dangerous.

Before anyone thinks that I am condoning drinking and driving, you need to know that this problem doesn't just affect habitual drunk drivers. In Indiana, you cannot be publicly intoxicated. Recently, *public intoxication* was construed to mean that you cannot even be a passenger in a car if you have been drinking[68]. The Indiana Supreme Court upheld the case of a woman who was ticketed for public intoxication after receiving a ride in her own car from a friend.

Earlier in the book, I discussed the situation of a man who was told it was illegal to give free rides to intoxicated individuals. Now, we find out that it is also illegal to receive a ride from a sober person. Being in your own car while intoxicated is considered *public intoxication* even if you don't cause any disturbance. The woman ticketed for public intoxication in Indiana was pulled over

---

68 http://newsandtribune.com/opinion/x971904054/HARBESON-Designate-PI-law-for-repeal

because her license plate light was out. If you cannot give the rides or receive them, it sounds like designated driving is what is illegal.

Someone should probably tell the major alcohol companies in the United States to discontinue their efforts to encourage the illegal practice of designated driving. In light of new regulations and their implications, they might want to change their messages. I often hear radio adverts promoting designated drivers. Anheuser-Busch even sponsored a designated driver program this year that bears remarkable similarities to the illegal program in Quincy, Illinois[69].

Just like the environmental vs. aesthetic issue of clotheslines, the current interpretation of public intoxication is a classic example of legislation and social agendas stepping on each other's toes, and the ordinary citizen is left wondering what he or she is supposed to do. The tragedy here is that, even when people are trying to be as responsible as possible, they are penalized. The next time a responsible adult wants to have an alcoholic beverage in public and then go home, they should not only call a cab, but they should also take a breathalyzer test before stepping into it.

The problem of not knowing whether you're over the legal limit isn't exactly clarified when the police give a person a breathalyzer test because the accuracy of the breathalyzer is unknown. If a person is caught violating the speed limit, they can

---

69 http://www.wrap.org/soberride/

question the radar gun since they can compare it to the speedometer in their car. In the case of noise violations and drunk driving charges, most of us just have to trust the police.

Even if you're a teetotaler, you are not immune to the craziness of the breathalyzer laws. In Indiana, your driver's license can be immediately revoked for refusing to submit to a breathalyzer test[70]. So, if you know you're not intoxicated while driving because you haven't even had an alcoholic beverage, you shouldn't have to worry about it, right? Not so fast.

I don't know about you, but I've dropped things onto the passenger floorboard a time or two while driving. After surveying the landscape for upcoming hazards, I've taken the chance at reaching way too far down to get the dropped item. After retrieving the item, I typically have to re-enter the proper lane of traffic. If a law enforcement officer happens to see me swerve in that manner, he or she could think I am intoxicated and pull me over. Let's say, even after talking to me, the officer asks me to submit to a field sobriety test just to be sure.

While I would usually be comfortable proving to the officer that I was not intoxicated, I would think twice about performing this test if I happened to be in front of my kids' school, or my church, or my boss's house. It's one thing to be witnessed by others being pulled over for speeding or not using your turn

---

70 http://www.in.gov/bmv/files/Drivers_Manual_Chapter_3.pdf

signal, but it's a completely different scenario for significant and influential people in your life to witness you walking the line or blowing into a machine. However, if you refuse to be humiliated in this manner in Indiana, "your driver's license will be confiscated and your driving privileges may be suspended for up to two years." Even my municipality has a code that reads "No person shall willfully fail or refuse to comply with any lawful order or direction of a police officer or Fire Department official."

This isn't meant to be a treatise against police, but I do acknowledge the possibility of a few bad cops being able to do a lot of unnecessary damage with this power. Most police aren't malevolent, but to simply trust them and blindly obey because they're uniformed is naive.

Laws that Overly-Criminalize

The punishment should fit the crime. That's what we've always been told. As a mother of young children, I have to make decisions every day about how to address certain behaviors. It is my job to decide which battles to engage and which to let go.

Many of the codes and laws that have been discussed in this book are overlooked. They are on the books but they are generally not enforced, and that is why they are so shocking to us when they are enforced. The same way I have to look at my children's behavior and decide what to address, our local government needs to look around our cities and decide what is worth fighting.

The fact that Marion, Indiana has what amounts to about seven pounds of municipal codes in the form of printed material doesn't seem to have made the town any nicer. I still see tall weeds. I still see rain-soaked mattresses in people's yards. I still see abandoned houses, and I still hear loud mufflers. It's probably the same situation in your town.

Every now and then, however, those in charge decide to crack down on someone. Maybe they are trying to use that person as an example to force compliance or maybe the violator irked someone at city hall. Either way, these stories tend to get our attention and cause outrage. They deserve our outrage because they are unjust; the punishments typically don't fit the crimes.

Most of us would probably agree that jail should be reserved for criminals. Do you consider a person a criminal if they don't sod their lawn? Some communities in Florida do. A man who couldn't afford to sod his lawn had ignored orders to do so in order to keep making his house payments, and he was sent to jail for it[71]. He was not permitted to be bailed out, either. He had to remain incarcerated until the lawn work was completed. How can a person pay for lawn work to be done if he or she is in jail not

---

71 http://www.tampabay.com/news/humaninterest/article847365.ece

making any money? It's worth noting that the jail he spent time in was overcrowded. I wonder why.

Nobody likes to put up with an unsightly lawn in his or her neighborhood. I agree that it's not fair for one person to work hard at maintaining their property while the chap next door starts a mini jungle. But, does it deserve jail time? Some people in Canton, Ohio think so[72]. The city council there looked into the possibility of jailing residents with tall grass on the second offense.

Unfortunately, those of us who have never been in jail judge those who have been. We think they must be drug addicts or child molesters. Not anymore. They just didn't mow their lawns often enough.

Here in Indiana, it has been a dry summer. We've only mowed our lawn twice in the last month. Some of our neighbors have mowed even less, and some of their weeds are growing kind of tall right now. But, I'm glad they don't send the homeowner to jail in my town. It's an elderly woman whose son mows for her. It's been over 90 degrees Fahrenheit for weeks now. I wouldn't want to force these people to choose between laboring in the sweltering heat and jail.

---

72 http://www.uslaw.com/library/Bad_Cops_&_Prosecutors/Canton_Ohio_Jail_Homeowners_Tall_Grass.php?item=148489

Over-criminalization is occurring in more serious ways than short jail stays for municipal code violations, though. Some people are being sent to prison for life for marijuana use[73]. Yet, alcohol-related deaths far outweigh anything associated with marijuana use[74]. Often, people sent to prison for non-violent marijuana convictions learn how to become *real* criminals while in prison. Then, when they get out, and may be unable to get jobs because they are convicted felons, they turn to more serious crimes to get by.

Some laws on the books are also overly-criminalizing normal adolescent behavior. We don't like to talk about it or admit it, but adolescents are curious sexually. They are learning about this aspect of themselves, and if they are not experimenting with it, they are at least discussing it with their peers.

A normal mode of communication for a lot of kids is texting. At this time, there are laws on the books outlawing sending sex-related messages. This is called *sexting* in the vernacular. Sometimes, these messages contain lewd pictures or videos. While I certainly don't endorse such behavior, I don't consider sex-related messages sent amongst minors to be worthy of labeling the offender a *child pornographer*.

---

[73] http://www.nola.com/crime/index.ssf/2011/05/fourth_marijuana_conviction_ge.html

[74] http://www.cdc.gov/mmwr/preview/mmwrhtml/mm5337a2.htm

Being convicted of child pornography can be disastrous to a young person. Besides being labeled with the biggest remaining taboo of our time, there is the possibility of being forced to register as a sex offender for life. Registered sex offenders have restrictions on where they can live and work. Some even have to put signs up labeling themselves like a modern day scarlet letter.

Being required to register as a sex offender has happened to many young men (and even women) in our country. Sometimes, they have simply sent sex-related text messages, had consensual sexual relations with someone slightly younger than themselves, or been involved in horseplay[75].

Recently, this happened to two 14-year-olds in New Jersey. "To make their friends laugh", they pulled down their pants and sat on two younger kids' heads. Now, they have to register as sex offenders for the rest of their lives unless their cases are overturned. Not that this behavior is in any way acceptable, but does the punishment really fit the crime?

Convenience Codes

A law of convenience is anything but convenient for those of us attempting to follow the rules. As far as I can tell, these laws only exist to make the job of law enforcement easier. Of course, we

---

[75] http://www.nj.com/news/index.ssf/2011/07/teens_sex_offenders_horseplay.html

are told that they are in place for our protection, but you can decide for yourself.

I grew up in Michigan. The winters were pretty cold. Oftentimes, on cold mornings, the first thing I would do after getting up was to start my car. Then, I would get ready for school. It took the same amount of time for my car to warm up as it did for me to shower, get dressed, eat breakfast (mom insisted), and primp.

I didn't know then, but what I was doing was illegal. And my parents probably didn't know they were contributing to the delinquency of a minor by allowing me to break the law like that. In many states it is illegal to leave a running vehicle unattended, even on your own property.

The stated reason for this is to keep your property safe. The argument is that a criminal will find a running vehicle too tempting and thefts are more likely to occur. However, shouldn't it be an individual's right to choose to risk his or her own property in that manner? No, because auto theft cases take up too many police resources[76]. Really, that's what it boils down to. If it were really about our protection, we should be able to decide for ourselves the level of protection we desire based on the perceived risks in our environment. Instead, it is about not bothering the police with complaints of theft when it's your fault you left your

---

76 http://www.kolotv.com/home/headlines/37057154.html

car running – not the thief's fault for stealing it. This reversal in our culture is amazing. We now blame the victims of crimes for enticing the criminals.

In a similar vein, my current city has an ordinance that requires you to register your bicycle with them. It mandates that the bicycle bear a reflective decal on the rear. The Chief of Police is responsible for issuing these licenses. They are to be renewed every two years at a cost of $.25. That's right – 12.5 cents per year.

The charge of such a nominal fee leads me to believe that they aren't requiring the registration of bicycles as a revenue source. Even if every resident in Marion had a bicycle, the city would only generate about $3,750 per year. I haven't seen the city budget, but I'm guessing that's pretty trivial. So, what is the reason behind mandating the registration of bicycles? Clearly, it's to prevent theft.

Bikes are stolen regularly, but that's not because they're not registered, it's because they're left outside without locks. I don't know if registering a bike wards off thieves or not. I do know that it makes less work for the police in tracking down the owners of recovered bicycles.

Currently, I don't own a bicycle. But, I've done a quick survey of my friends, and none of them have registered their bicycles. In fact, as I suspected, they weren't aware of this requirement. I have a feeling that some police officers might not even be aware of it, and I highly doubt the Chief of Police would appreciate every bicycle owner in Marion knocking on his door to register their bikes in an odd turn of sudden compliance.

My hypothesis is that they overlook requiring bicycles to be registered because the registration process is more of a hassle than handling stolen bike calls. To test whether this code is legitimate, I had my friend attempt to register her family's bicycles. I wrote about her experiences in Field Journal E.

The ultimate example of a law in place for police convenience comes to us from my friends who own rental properties in a St. Louis, Missouri suburb. They were told they had to remove a fence on their property. The reason? It was too tall to allow the police to chase fleeing suspects. Evidently the police didn't think the suspects would have any trouble getting over the fence, though. But, police convenience trumps property rights in this case. What if the property owners and renters don't prefer to have police chases occurring in their yard? Maybe they should build the fence so tall that nobody can scale it – suspect or police.

America's Idol – Safety

We live in a safe society. Our country is so safe that we have been lulled into believing that every accident is preventable. We covet safety. This attitude has led to a lot of paranoia and government regulation.

Sometimes tragedies occur. When they do, the general public almost always looks to the government to solve the problem or keep it from happening again. Usually, some Congressperson at the state or national level writes up a bill that, if in force at the time of the accident or crime, putatively would have prevented said accident/crime from occurring.

Well-intentioned though they are, most of these reactionary laws are useless at best and criminal at worst. *Caylee's Law* is the unofficial name for the bills on the table in several states that would make it a felony for a parent to fail to report a missing child[77]. This is a reaction to the high-profile case of Caylee Anthony's death. Her mother, Casey, was acquitted of murdering her, but the public remains skeptical because of her bizarre behavior, including not reporting her daughter missing for 31 days. A lot of the general public are outraged by her not being found guilty. This is their way of keeping something like this from happening again. But, even if it passes, it won't punish Casey, and it won't save Caylee.

The only thing that Caylee's Law will do is criminalize good parents. If someone is going to murder their child, they aren't motivated not to simply because of this proposed law. Neglectful parents aren't suddenly motivated to be good parents when additional behaviors are considered felonies. However, good

---

77 http://en.wikipedia.org/wiki/Caylee%27s_Law

parents sometimes trust their kids to be gone for a few hours and might not even realize they're not precisely where they said they would be.

Caylee's Law will most-likely include a vague guideline about reporting the child missing *in a timely manner*. If your 16-year-old goes to the mall and leaves his or her cell phone in the car, they could be *missing* for an entire day. I know I could lose myself in the mall at that age.

What if you don't believe in allowing your kids to have cell phones? In that case, the kids could be construed as being *missing* during any amount of time that you, as a parent, have chosen to allow them freedom away from the house. All it takes is a paranoid parent to see your kids out and about and an enthusiastic district attorney to make it happen[78]. You could be a felon.

When I was growing up nobody had cell phones. There wasn't nearly as much checking in with parents as there is today. You would think this extra checking in would lead to less paranoia, but it has succeeded it making parents more paranoid when they don't get the call or answered text. My friends and I had to find a pay phone. Sometimes, if we were out of change, we called our parents collect. Some parents would decline the call because they knew we were just checking in and they could hear our voices say our names on the other end. That was enough for them – just to

---

78 http://freerangekids.wordpress.com/2011/07/11/guest-post-caylees-law-could-make-me-a-criminal/

know that we were still breathing. If you're reading this and you have no idea what I'm talking about, go ask someone at least 30 years old.

Keeping us *safe* and *preventing crime* has already forced me to give up my cold remedy of choice – Sudafed. Yeah, I can still buy it, but it's a huge hassle, and I can't be bothered to endure the questioning stares that accompany its purchase. Sudafed, which contains ephedrine, can be used as one of the ingredients to make methamphetamine (meth). Since meth use and production has become such a problem, the government has made restrictive laws on the purchase of products containing ephedrine, like Sudafed.

In Indiana, a woman was arrested for purchasing more than three grams of ephedrine in a seven-day period[79]. The law, meant to catch criminals who make meth, has been enforced in this case even though she was using the medicine for legal purposes. Here is a quote from Nina Alexander, the county prosecutor in this case:

> *Just as with any law, the public has the responsibility to know what is legal and what is not, and ignorance of the law is no excuse. I'm simply enforcing the law as it was written.*

---

[79] http://tribstar.com/local/x46868452/Wabash-Valley-woman-didn-t-realize-second-cold-medicine-purchase-violated-drug-laws

Here we have a woman in rural Indiana who was able to prove that she was using the medicine legally, and she still faces criminal action because of the way the law is written. So, in addition to being a deterrent to meth production, this law functions as a way of criminalizing legal medication. Instead of law enforcement officials investigating the purchases individually and using their judgment, it allows prosecutors to knowingly press charges against innocent people. I thought this law was meant to keep the general public safe by restricting harmful drug use. Nope, it just makes criminals out of grandmas trying to buy medicine for their grandkids.

The idol of safety has also led to insanity in our schools. Why aren't our kids keeping up with those in other countries? Maybe it's because going to school is quite similar to going to prison now.

In the name of safety, a couple of schools in Texas started handing out radio frequency tracking devices to all pupils[80]. Generally speaking, it's probably not a good idea to tether innocent people. Whether it's intentional or not, kids get the same message that other people get when they are tethered – that they're under house arrest.

Just in case tracking devices don't seem prison-y enough for you, a school in Texas is issuing prison jumpsuits to students

---

80 http://abclocal.go.com/ktrk/story?section=news/local&id=7717793

who violate the dress code[81]. The decision was made in order to make sure the students are focused on education instead of on clothes, but these jumpsuits will most likely stand out more than their unacceptable clothes.

The desire to protect children from unsafe food has prompted one school district in Chicago to ban all outside food[82]. There will be no more paper bag lunches at Chicago's Little Village Academy public school because the school claims that the students are healthier and safer when they buy lunch from the school. A school in Tucson, Arizona still allows brown paper bag lunches, but they check to make sure it's healthy – no white flour, refined sugar, or other processed foods are allowed.

Keeping school grounds safe and orderly has led to one Virginia middle school banning all physical contact[83]. The banned physical contact includes handshakes, high fives, and hugs. I suppose they are assuming that students are incapable of knowing the difference between wanted and unwanted touch, which is something we teach children at a very young age.

While these school-related rule infractions aren't always illegal, many of them sure make the students feel like convicts and

---

81 http://www.foxnews.com/story/0,2933,396362,00.html

82 http://news.yahoo.com/blogs/lookout/chicago-school-bans-homemade-lunches-latest-national-food-20110411-092947-380.html

83 http://www.washingtonpost.com/wp-dyn/content/article/2007/06/17/AR2007061701179.html

criminals. And, sometimes they are illegal. School police officers are writing criminal citations to students for behavior that would have warranted detention in previous years[84]. Tickets are even issued to elementary school students and results in a "dangerous melding of education and criminal justice that too often and too early introduces children to the law enforcement arena, often a precursor to prison as an adult."

In 2009, twenty-five students aged 11-15 were arrested and taken to jail for calling in bomb threats. Just kidding. They were taken to jail for a food fight[85]. They were charged with reckless conduct. Are we really so concerned about safety and order that we are ready to criminalize our children for normal adolescent behavior? One mother lamented the incident:

> *My children have to appear in court. They were handcuffed, slammed in a wagon, had their mug shots taken and treated like real criminals. They're all scared. You never know how children will be impacted by that. I was all for some other kind of punishment, but not jail. Who hasn't had a food fight?*

Over the top school safety measures have led to most zero tolerance policies related to weapons. Even a kindergarten boy

---

84 http://www.texastribune.org/texas-education/public-education/school-district-cops-ticket-thousands-of-students/

85 http://www.nytimes.com/2009/11/11/us/11foodfight.html?_r=1

with a Nerf gun got suspended[86]. And what does the principal have to say about that? "It's not too harsh of a punishment and we want to make sure all of our students are safe." Keeping kids safe probably shouldn't involve scaring good kids into thinking they're troublemakers.

Keeping us safe through regulation takes away freedom. If we continue to idolize safety, we will succeed in restricting freedoms, labeling good parents as criminals, and encouraging paranoia. Mendel Klein, a pediatric occupational therapist and blogger summarizes it best:

> *Passing laws might boost politicians' profiles. Petitioning for these laws might make us feel good. But reacting in these ways also boosts our fear and paranoia, while making our children no safer. It's time to vote nay on these retroactive, post-mortem, feel-good laws, no matter whose name is attached[87].*

Many of the topics I've discussed in this book can boil down to our idolization of safety. We expect products we buy to be safe, even at garage sales. This has gotten so out of control that even very safe products are being recalled. Drop side cribs are only one example of many[88]. A child is more likely to get hurt in a car or falling down the stairs than in a drop side crib. Truthfully, I

---

86 http://www.9news.com/news/story.aspx?storyid=156961&catid=339

87 http://freerangekids.wordpress.com/2011/07/25/leibys-law-would-not-have-saved-leiby/

don't bother to keep up with recalled items. Much like reading the municipal codes, I will probably discover more than I want to know.

Outdated Laws

I've ranted at length about laws that are useless because they are not enforced. Truthfully, I don't want all of them to be enforced, especially if they're outdated.

When I was an addictions counselor, I worked in a residential facility. We had a rule that clients had to use blue pens and staff had to use black pens. Any client caught using a black pen could get into trouble. The rule was in place to avoid any client attempting to forge their counselor's signature on important documents – like discharge papers and treatment plans.

I didn't enforce this rule. I chose to ignore it because it was outdated. By the time I left, counselors were no longer using black pens at all. Everything was done on computers, including digital signatures for all clinical activities. Even the clients signed documents digitally in their counselor's offices. But, when a client arrived, they were given a list of rules, and staff were expected to enforce all of them, regardless of their efficacy. Some staff did just that.

---

88 http://freerangekids.wordpress.com/2010/12/17/some-non-mainstream-thoughts-on-the-crib-recall/

If this analogy is applied to law enforcement, we find that people can potentially get punished for something that doesn't matter at all. In my town, there is a municipal code that forbids a non-functioning refrigerator from being on anyone's property unless the door has been removed from the frame. This is a prevalent law throughout America. Although the law doesn't say so, this is to prevent children from playing in and getting stuck in old refrigerators and suffocating. This actually used to happen, but that was when refrigerator doors locked from the outside. Any child over two or so could easily bust out of a modern refrigerator with its magnetic doors. Even the CPSC indicates that this recommendation applies to old-style refrigerators,[89] but that isn't indicated in the municipal code. Since it isn't indicated, a person could receive a citation for this offense, even though the result doesn't make anybody safer. In fact, it would be more dangerous to have a functioning old-style refrigerator than a non-functioning new one.

When I was in high school, I was on the student council. This is the closest I've come in my life to being involved in government. We were responsible for scheduling school dances and booking the disc jockey (DJ). There was a standard contract in place, written before my time, that the DJ would sign.

---

89 http://www.cpsc.gov/cpscpub/pubs/5072.html

One of the student council members bothered to read the contract once (it actually wasn't me) and pointed out something interesting – it was a breach of contract for the DJ to play the song "Mony Mony". The song was a hit for Tommy James & the Shondells in 1968, but Billy Idol remade it in 1981, with a live version being recorded and popularized in 1987. In the 1980s, "people would shout a certain formulaic (and usually obscene) sentence in the two bars following each line" when the song was played[90]. However, neither my classmates nor I knew of this tradition until we read about it in the DJ's contract. At that point, the school had to continue to ban playing the song since we now knew what kind of trouble we could cause at the dance. However, if it had been removed in a timely manner (or never put in the contract to begin with), the tradition may have died out long ago. By now, no high-school student wants to hear that song, anyway.

Revenue-Generating Laws

If a government entity needs to generate revenue, a good place to start would be to outlaw something. That way, citations can be issued in bulk and the problem is solved. Of course, the only problem with this is that a need for money isn't a good reason to pass a law.

Seat belt laws are a good example of this. Wearing a seat belt is definitely the prudent thing to do for your own safety. But,

---

90 http://en.wikipedia.org/wiki/Mony_Mony

it's also a good thing to do if you want to avoid paying a fine. States have even admitted that being cash strapped is one of their motivations for mandating seat belt use[91].

Here's another problem with passing a law to generate revenue: If people actually obey the law, sufficient revenue will not be generated. At that point, they need to come up with something else to forbid to make ends meet. This way of thinking has the potential to be a real juggernaut in removing freedom of choice.

Conclusion

We have too many laws, and many of them are flawed. If any of our Founding Fathers had been cryogenically frozen, and if we had a way of waking them up from suspended animation, I think they would awake to a country they don't recognize as free. They might hang out for a while and try to live within the laws of the land, and then get frustrated and and decide to start another revolution. I wouldn't put it past them – especially that Aaron Burr character. Rumor has it he was good with a gun.

---

91 http://seattletimes.nwsource.com/html/nationworld/2008705249_apseatbeltlaws.html

CONTINUING THE EXPERIMENT

The United States has often been referred to as the great experiment. The National Center for Constitutional Studies explains the ways in which the American Experiment was made distinct by the Founding Fathers[92].

First, the great American experiment was based on liberty. America is supposed to be "the land of the free and the home of the brave." If we are truly *free*, we should be able to eat salt if we want to. Common sense would tell us that a free person would be able to grow a garden in his or her yard or set up a lemonade stand. Unfortunately, this no longer the case.

---

92 http://www.nccs.net/articles/ril71.html

Today, any person reading this book realizes that he or she could receive copious fines (and possibly jail time in some areas) for violating city ordinances. I hope I have demonstrated successfully that even the most well-intentioned individual can find him- or herself on the wrong side of the law in today's society. Let me ask you. Are we really the home of the free? The United States comprises 5% of the world's population and 25% of the world's prisoners[93]. James Whitman, a professor at Yale expounds on this:

> *People who commit nonviolent crimes in the rest of the world are less likely to receive prison time and certainly less likely to receive long sentences. The United States is, for instance, the only advanced country that incarcerates people for minor property crimes like passing bad checks. Efforts to combat illegal drugs play a major role in explaining long prison sentences in the United States as well. In 1980, there were about 40,000 people in American jails and prisons for drug crimes. These days, there are almost 500,000.*

In order for this great experiment to be a success, we must focus on liberty, and resist the urge to legislate. We can't legislate our way into utopia. We can't expect those things that annoy us to

---

[93] http://www.nytimes.com/2008/04/23/world/americas/23iht-23prison.12253738.html

be illegal, but then have everything legal that we want to do. Mounds of legislation will work against us in the end. The bills that pass through Congress are often so bulky that the Congresspeople admit to not reading them before voting[94]. That, of all things, should be illegal.

Secondly, the Founding Fathers responsible for this great experiment recognized the normal human desire for power and the tendency to abuse it. Certain measures are written into our Constitution to prevent the abuse of power, such as the separation of powers into the branches of government that all have a way of checking each other[95].

This isn't always the case, but I can't rule out the possibility of vanity being the reason for some of the laws of the land. Elected officials want to be remembered for something the way the rest of us do. They want their work to *make a difference*. Often, this results in them lauding the legislation they voted for that keeps us all safer by outlawing smoking, texting, raw milk, or sundry other *offenses*. These laws often do not keep us safer, but serve to take away our freedoms and choices.

---

[94] http://hillbuzz.org/2009/02/13/senators-admit-they-are-not-going-to-read-the-trillion-dollar-spending-bill-before-voting-on-it/

[95] http://en.wikipedia.org/wiki/Separation_of_powers_under_the_United_States_Constitution

I really want to teach my children to trust the police. It's just that it's getting increasingly difficult to hold that position when the police are expected to enforce laws that I don't agree with. Besides that, police are given tools to help them fight crime, but many of them can be abused and used against law-abiding citizens. The Michigan Court of Appeals ruled in 2008 that the police don't need a warrant to use drug sniffing dogs around the outside perimeter of your house[96].

I'm not as concerned about my neighbors possessing drugs as I am about the police abusing their power. The natural human desire for power and the tendency to abuse it doesn't take a break just because someone is labeled as a *public servant*. Even though searching for drugs around someone's house is meant to catch criminals, it is done without probable cause. If there were probable cause, they would just get the search warrant.

Today, our legislators always talk about working together to *get things done*. Bipartisanship is lauded as a virtue worthy of re-election. Maybe it would be better for everyone if they continued to battle each other so that not so much got done. It seems like what they accomplish when they *get something done* is pass monumental amounts of legislation that continue to restrict

---

[96] http://www.mlive.com/news/index.ssf/2008/05/court_drug_dogs_can_sniff_outs.html

freedoms and make it harder to recognize that we live in the supposed land of the free.

This attitude starts at the federal level and trickles all the way down to your city council. Rules have gotten so out of control that I'm not allowed to smile for my driver's license picture in Indiana[97]. Granted, it's difficult to keep a smile on my face after enduring a day at the Bureau of Motor Vehicles, but I still feel chipper when it's about time to leave. Since I'm not allowed to smile, my driver's license picture looks a lot like how I felt that day – overwhelmed with bureaucracy.

When I started this book, I also started a blog at technicallythatsillegal.com. This has motivated people to send me all kinds of articles for inclusion on the blog. I've spent the last few weeks reading about people getting arrested for failing to use their turn signals, popping pimples in public, feeding birds, saving animals, and wearing costumes. It never stops. I invite you to join the insanity by following my blog. I hope the blog accomplishes the task of convincing people that we don't need more regulation. We need less.

If, like me, you're tired of being overwhelmed with bureaucracy, maybe we should engage in some other experiments together. In order to continue this great experiment known as The

---

97 http://www.theindychannel.com/news/18226101/detail.html

United States of America, we need to put the focus back on liberty. Let's experiment with what happens if we begin to balk at the tendency to want the government to fix our problems. Right now, we want the government to fix our schools, keep our streets safe, tell us what to eat, prevent tragedy, and be good parents.

Regular individuals like you and I generally have a better idea about how to tackle big problems like education, violence, and parenting from the community level. The fact is that the government is too big for its britches. It cannot be expected to tackle the problem of our crumbling educational system if it cannot maintain competence in other important areas, like the prescription drug approval process. Civic involvement has taken a back seat to expecting governmental control. The government is largely responsible for this attitude because of the way it discourages private citizens from making a difference in areas of benevolence outlined in chapter two.

I want us to experiment with overlooking some of our neighbor's faults (and assume that they're doing the same). I want us to use our negotiation skills to solve problems rather than calling code enforcement. In some areas, the concept of working things out amongst ourselves is foreign. This line of thinking is reinforced by the fact that it is becoming increasingly popular to mandate that people report crimes.

I don't think very many towns would be worse off without the municipal code. City ordinances are rarely the motivation behind a person keeping their property nice and clean. Taxation is definitely not the motivation. Property taxes are just one more example of the many ways we are given mixed messages as a result of too much government. The ordinances tell us to have our property in ship shape, and property taxes serve as a disincentive for that. As we improve our property, the value goes up, and the taxes go up, too.

One important aspect of this ongoing experiment in American life is the ways in which we judge one another. The next time you see someone taking a field sobriety test or having code enforcement show up at their house, take a moment to put yourself in their shoes. Recall at that moment that you probably haven't registered your dogs or obtained the proper cover for your outdoor fire pit. You may have ridden a motorcycle and violated the city noise ordinance. You might even have committed an audacious illegal act of kindness. Regardless of the situation, let's experiment with avoiding labeling a person as a *criminal*. As I've demonstrated in this book, there's probably a little *criminal* in all of us.

Right now, it is becoming increasingly obvious that those outside of the United States don't trust our government's leadership. They see it as self-serving, and that's the nature of the beast known as government[98]. As I recall, we're supposed to have a government of, by, and for the people, not the other way around.

Several years ago I thought about the issues in this book totally differently. I remember hearing about the Bush administration's warrantless wiretapping and wondering why people were protesting when Attorney General Alberto Gonzalez gave public talks on the issue. I thought, like many people, that there's no reason to object to surveillance if you've got nothing to hide. Then I remembered the Constitution. The fourth amendment reads:

> *The right of the people to be secure in their persons, houses, papers, and effects, against unreasonable searches and seizures, shall not be violated, and no Warrants shall issue, but upon probable cause, supported by Oath or affirmation, and particularly describing the place to be searched, and the persons or things to be seized[99].*

It's interesting to note here that the Federal Bureau of Investigation (FBI) now considers constitutionalists to be potential terrorists[100]. One FBI flier distributed in Phoenix lists

---

98 http://www.heritage.org/research/commentary/2007/07/the-american-experiment

99 http://caselaw.lp.findlaw.com/data/constitution/amendment04/

100 http://www.fbi.gov/stats-services/publications/terrorism-2002-2005

constitutionalists in the same breath as skinheads and violent anti-abortion extremists as people to report to the Joint Terrorism Task Force[101].

If the government can spy on us without cause and if they consider me a potential terrorist, they might just show up at my house, look around, and find more than they bargained for –unsorted recycling, a fire burning after 7:00 p.m., and a baby in a drop-side crib. They might have to call for backup on this one.

---

[101] http://thepatriotsnews.com/FBI_Flyer%5B1%5D.pdf

FIELD JOURNAL A

Obtaining a Mesh Cover for Burning Barrel

I don't know the specific numbers, but quite a few people in this town have burning barrels. They are not used to burn garbage but yard waste. My back yard even has a small concrete slab, which was in place before we moved in, for the purpose of housing the barrel.

When we obtained our barrel nothing was mentioned about having a cover for it, and to my knowledge, none of my neighbors have covers. However, the municipal code states that we must have one. An adequate container for burning is defined as:

> *A non-combustible 55 gallon barrel or drum sufficiently vented to induce adequate primary combustion air with enclosed sides, a bottom and a mesh covering with openings no larger than 1/4" square.*

In order to obtain the proper mesh covering, I went to a local farm supply store. The worker at the store indicated that they did have some wire mesh, but that they were not big enough to cover the typical 55-gallon drum. She gave me the name and number of a steel company in the county.

The worker indicated that the store didn't carry the mesh covers because they are "not an every day item, which makes it too expensive to stock." In other words, nobody but me is looking for one of these things so they don't want to waste shelf space on it. If this ordinance were enforced, the store would sell plenty of them.

I called the number for the steel company that the woman at the store gave me. I told him I needed a mesh cover for my barrel. He knew what I was talking about, but said that they would have to "get it ready." I got the impression that they don't sell these very often because he had to calculate the price and cut the steel specifically to size.

Another interesting thing is that he told me I would have to buy two of them. One of them would only be $10, but they have a $20 minimum public sale. I would have assumed that there would be tons of extras of these lying around since people are forced to buy two of them at the only known store in the county for procuring one of these. But, that's not the case because I'm the only person bothering to do this.

When I went to go get the steel mesh, I realized he was cutting pieces that had holes of 3/4" rather than the required 1/4". When I asked him if he had anything smaller, he showed me some thin and rather flimsy material that would probably last about an hour when used as a cover for a burning barrel. He said the 3/4" is standard for use as a fire covering. I paid for the materials, but decided to go to several other stores to look for the exact item.

I went to another farm supply store in town and also a hardware store. Neither had 1/4" mesh steel grate of the type needed for covering burning barrels. I guess I will continue to be in violation of this code. I conclude that this ordinance is too difficult to follow if nobody in town, including a steel company, carries what I need to be in compliance. I hope I don't get a citation this fall when we're burning leaves. But, if anyone wants one, I've got an extra useless steel cover.

FIELD JOURNAL B

Aims

In this experiment, I am testing whether either of the motorcycles I own violate my city's noise ordinance. The noise ordinance reads:

> *No person shall cause the sound pressure level of the noise emitted during the operation of a light motor vehicle to exceed 80 DBA in speed zones of 45 miles per hour or less within the city. The sound pressure level measurement shall be made at a distance of not less than 15 feet from the edge of the lane of travel of the violator.*

Materials

1. Small notebook
2. Mechanical pencil
3. RadioShack Analog Sound Level Meter model 33-4050.
4. Tape measure
5. 2003 Harley-Davidson Dyna Wide Glide motorcycle fitted with aftermarket exhaust pipes
6. 2011 Suzuki Boulevard S40 motorcycle fitted with a Harley-Davidson stock, baffled exhaust pipe
7. Husband

Method

To begin, I measured off a distance of 15 feet from the left and right side of each motorcycle. My husband started each one in succession, and I took readings with the decibel meter. The following readings were recorded in the notebook using the mechanical pencil: exhaust side idle, exhaust side revving, non-exhaust side idle, and non-exhaust side revving.

Results

When testing the Harley-Davidson, I stood 15 feet away and took several different measurements. From the side with no exhaust pipes, the motorcycle registered at 76 decibels when idling. When my husband revved the motor, it registered just over

100 decibels. When I moved to the side with the exhaust pipes, the idle measurement was 79 decibels, and well over 100 decibels when revving the motor.

When testing the Suzuki, I stood 15 feet away and took several different measurements. From the side with no exhaust pipes, the motorcycle registered at 63 decibels when idling. When my husband revved the motor, it registered at 83 decibels. When I moved to the side with the exhaust pipe, the idle measurement was 62 decibels and 82 decibels when revving the motor.

Discussion

It was no surprise at all that the Harley-Davidson motorcycle is in violation of the noise ordinance considering its aftermarket exhaust pipes. I am just thankful that we usually ride it outside of town and don't engage in unnecessary idling or revving.

I was a little bit surprised that the Suzuki was in violation of the noise ordinance while revving considering that it's fitted with a baffled, unaltered, stock Harley-Davidson muffler. This means that this motorcycle is in violation of the noise ordinance during acceleration. It doesn't seem like a very loud motorcycle to me. It would surely be quieter than the Harley-Davidson motorcycle that originally had the muffler I am using on this Suzuki, but the numbers don't lie.

One of my theories about why this ordinance is not enforced is because the police themselves use patrol motorcycles at times. If my little 650 cc Suzuki with a baffled muffler is in violation of this code, then surely the large motorcycles police officers use, which are usually Harley-Davidsons, are also in violation. So, why even have such an ordinance in the first place? That's a good question.

For those who are interested, my infant son registered at 85 decibels from 15 feet away when he was tired, cranky, and ready for a nap.

FIELD JOURNAL C

Aims

In this experiment, I am testing the number of vehicles that violate the noise ordinance as they drive past my house.

The ordinance reads:

> No person shall cause the sound pressure level of the noise emitted during the operation of a light motor vehicle to exceed 80 DBA in speed zones of 45 miles per hour or less within the city. The sound pressure level

measurement shall be made at a distance of not less than 15 feet from the edge of the lane of travel of the violator.

Materials

1. Small notebook

2. Mechanical pencil

3. RadioShack Analog Sound Level Meter model 33-4050.

4. Tape measure

Method

To begin, I measured off a distance of 15 feet from the southbound (near) lane beside my house. This was approximately 3 feet from my front step, so the reported measurements were taken from a distance of 18 feet in order to avoid conspicuousness while I sat on the step. The northbound (far) lane of traffic was 24 feet from the decibel meter. The meter was placed with the microphone toward the street. Measurements were noted in the notebook using the pencil.

Results

In three separate observation sessions, five out of 84 vehicles violated the city noise ordinance. Two were motorcycles and the others were a Chevrolet Trailblazer, a Chevrolet Metro, and a Nissan Sentra. This amounts to 6% of vehicles violating the noise ordinance.

Eight of the 84 vehicles registered at over 75 decibels, indicating that they might have been in violation of the ordinance had I been 15 feet away rather than 18, which is how it is stated in the code. The vehicles that came close to violating the noise ordinance were a Chevrolet Corsica, a Ford F-150, a Dodge Grand Caravan with squeaky breaks, a Chrysler PT Cruiser with loud music, and four unidentified motorcycles. If these vehicles are included among the percentage of violators, the total would be 15.5% (13/84). Fifty percent of motorcycles violated the city ordinance.

The following a pie graph provides a visual interpretation of the final results:

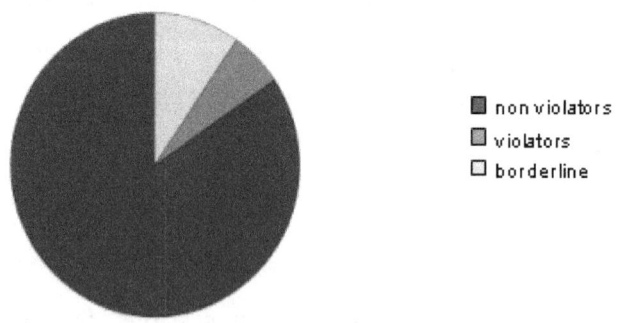

Discussion

I didn't catch as many violators as I thought I would, but a 6-15.5% noise ordinance violator rate is still pretty significant.

While I was waiting for traffic to go by, I noticed that the ambient sound level was registering at 74 with no traffic going by. This was a result of the cicadas. They could very well have been violating the city noise ordinance if the microphone had been pointed directly at them from a distance of 15 feet. If cicadas are potentially capable of breaking the city's noise ordinance, then perhaps it would be appropriate to re-think the practicality of this rule, which is never enforced, anyway.

FIELD JOURNAL D

Registering My Cats

I need to be in compliance with the following code:

The owner of every dog or cat shall purchase a license annually for such dog or cat. The cost of the license shall be $2 for each altered dog or cat and $3 for each unaltered dog or cat. The issuance of such licenses shall be administered by the Controller's Department.

My quest to register my cats started with a visit to the filing cabinet. I still keep a large filing cabinet for filing insurance quotes, bank statements, medical records, etc. Among the contents of my cabinet are veterinarian records. I have avoided sorting those records after several moves because each veterinarian has a different system of record keeping and it just got too confusing.

After a long battle with the file on my cats, I discovered that their rabies vaccinations were out of date. They have to be up to date in order to register with the city, so I called the veterinarian to schedule these vaccinations.

After much fanfare getting them into their travel cages, the cats were taken to the veterinarian and given their rabies vaccinations. The total for the two cats was $50.50 plus tax.

Then, I called City Hall to ask about registering my cats. When I asked them what I had to do, there was a long silence. I asked them if registering pets was required, and they said that it was "a good idea."

They transferred me to the Code Enforcement office. The municipal code online stated that pets should be registered with the Controller, so I assumed that's where I would be directed next. However, the code enforcement office told me to register them with Animal Care and Control, instead.

When I called Animal Care and Control during regular business hours, I was given a message that said to call back during regular business hours. I called at 4:00 p.m. on a Thursday. Their message stated that they were open from 1:00 p.m. to 5:00 p.m. Tuesday through Saturday. But, at least I got their address.

With the address in hand, I programmed my GPS to direct me to Animal Care and Control. I brought with me my two recently obtained rabies tags and proof that my cats are *altered*. I arrived and registered my animals without incident.

To my surprise, the worker actually knew what I was talking about, although I was not asked to supply any documentation. The fact that the animals have to be vaccinated against rabies does not need to be proven, and neither does the fact that they have been *altered*, even though there is a price difference for an *unaltered* animal.

When I left, I was given a certificate to prove that my cats had been registered. I read it when I got home. To my dismay, the certificate read that I had paid for the city registration of two domestic short-hair *dogs*.

FIELD JOURNAL E

Registering a Bicycle

Since I don't own any bicycles, I had a friend attempt to register hers. The bicycle ordinances in my town read accordingly:

> *No person who resides within the city shall ride or propel a bicycle on any street or upon any public path set aside for the exclusive use of bicycles unless such bicycle has been licensed and a reflectorized decal license is attached thereto as provided herein.*
>
> *The application for a bicycle license and a reflectorized decal license shall be made upon a form provided by the city and shall be made to the Chief of Police. A biennial*

license fee of $.25 shall be paid to the city before each license is granted.

The Chief of Police, upon receiving a proper application, may issue bicycle licenses which shall be effective on and after May 1 of each odd-numbered year.

(A)The Chief of Police shall issue a reflectorized decal license bearing the expiration date, the name of this city and the license number assigned to the bicycle.

(B)The reflectorized decal license shall be firmly attached to the rear mudguard or frame of the bicycle for which it was issued and shall be plainly visible from the rear.

(C)No person shall remove a reflectorized decal license from a bicycle before that license expires except upon a transfer of ownership or if the bicycle is dismantled and no longer operated upon any city street.

The Chief of Police shall inspect each bicycle before licensing it and shall refuse a license for any bicycle which he or she determines is in unsafe mechanical condition.

My friend's first order of business was to call the Chief of Police. Even though we suspected he wasn't specifically in charge of bicycle registration, this is what the code said to do. When she called the chief's office, she was transferred to the front desk. At that point, she encountered someone's voice mail, and left a message indicating that she wanted information about how to register her bicycles with the city.

When she received a return call later that day, the woman on the other end was very friendly. She told her that the Chief of Police isn't responsible for registering bicycles. She told my friend that registering bicycles is a service that the city offers and it is currently voluntary. There is also no longer a fee associated with the service and no inspection needs to be done. With this information, my friend decided not to go forward with the registration process.

As far as I can tell, there should not be any bicycle ordinances on the books in my town. The only part of the code that is still correct is that the city will issue you a decal. However, the parts that no longer reflect what the code says are who issues the decals, how much the decals cost, the fact that no inspection is required, and the fact that the decals are no longer mandatory.

"A lot of times when you first start out on a project you think, This is never going to be finished. But then it is, and you think, Wow, it wasn't even worth it."

- Jack Handey in The Lost Deep Thoughts

www.ingramcontent.com/pod-product-compliance
Lightning Source LLC
Chambersburg PA
CBHW060859170526
45158CB00001B/424